WE ADOPTED!

A COLLECTION OF DOG RESCUE TALES

DANIEL**BOEY**

 Marshall Cavendish
Editions

TO HOCK

"I miss you more today than yesterday but not as much as tomorrow"

C O N T

E N T S

It's so easy to say 'I love dogs' if you're talking about fluffy perfect dogs. When you're able to love a dog that isn't necessarily beautiful, then you love a dog. Ignorance perpetuates rejection, abandonment, overpopulation.

"

LYA BATTLE
FOUNDER, TERRITORIO DE ZAGUATES
(TERRITORY OF THE STRAYS)
COSTA RICA

AUTHOR'S MESSAGE
#DoingItDoggieStyle

Not many people know of my intense love for dogs. I have never publically spoken about it, even to close friends, although my late dog Ah Hock was featured posthumously in both my earlier books as well as in *8 Days* and numerous articles. So imagine my surprise when dog-loving creatives starting emerging from the woodwork after I adopted Leia. Real, genuine dog lovers, not dog snobs who profess publicly to love all dogs when they actually mean pedigrees, who turn their sophisticated designer noses up at mongrels and rescues.

Hock passed in 1991, and it's taken me the better part of twenty-six years before I could bring myself to embrace another canine in my life. I welcomed Leia into my life during a particularly turbulent period. When I asked for a hand, God gave me a paw. And how that paw has changed me.

Many think they are helping dogs that they adopt but more often than not, in reality, it is really us humans that have been rescued by our four-legged children.

The idea for this book was sparked when I worked on the SPCA Tux For Tails fundraiser with creative director Brandon Barker. We conceptualised a fashion shoot starring fourteen beautiful rescue dogs and five dog-loving Singaporean models for the souvenir magazine and the runway show.

We chose to tell these modern, real life fairy tales of doggie adoption through the medium of photography, and produced a series of stunning editorial spreads. Looking at the pictures, no one would have guessed the canine models were once abused, neglected, crippled or abandoned. These are some of the most incredible comeback stories, tales of resilience, forgiveness, trust, love, human cruelty, greed and miracle rebounds, with a life or two saved along the way

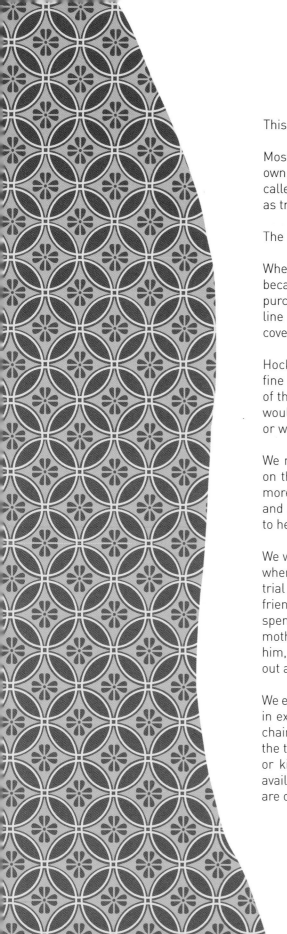

This book was spawned from that labour of love.

Most of the dogs featured in this book have been through their own personal Hell. Every single one at the hands of a species called Humans. And they have all bounced back and remain as trusting and as compassionate and loving as ever.

The empathy in animals is something we can all learn from.

When I was in Secondary 2, Satini Flame Hawk Forrell became the latest addition to join the Boey clan. He was purchased from 'a responsible breeder' and came from a line of championship dogs. He arrived unceremoniously in a covered plastic basket so shallow he could not even stand up.

Hock was not allowed indoors, which the family believed was fine because we had a huge back room which ran the breadth of the house. This was converted into his living quarters. He would sit dismally outside watching the family as we dined or watched television.

We moved our lives outside to accommodate him. We lazed on the garden furniture at the patio so that we could spend more time with him. I remember sneaking out the back door and sleeping in his kennel at night because it broke my heart to hear him cry himself to sleep.

We were first-time dog owners, and none the wiser. In a time when the internet did not exist, everything was done through trial and error or in consultation with more knowledgable friends. Hock had an attack of ticks and fleas, and the family spent countless hours pulling them off his body. Our hapless mother shopped for his food from the local market, bathed him, nursed him and kept him company whilst everyone was out at school.

We engaged a trainer for Hock. He was someone who believed in exerting dominance over his charges, and used the choke chain – which, I guess, was the norm in the early 80s. He was the type of trainer who thought nothing of jerking and pulling or kicking the dogs. Sadly, even with so much information available on the net, such trainers still exist today and there are owners who continue to believe in such methods.

There is a very clear, thick line between disciplining and hurting your dog.

There are many schools of thought with regards to doggie care. I will forever be haunted by the memory of how we had failed Hock, and have chosen to bring Leia up the humane way.

This book contains the stories of owners who never gave up on their dogs. I have been regaled with tales of senior dogs on the brink of death, dogs with several broken legs, blind dogs, crippled canines... all of whom have been heartlessly thrown out, yet rescued and nursed back to health by their saviours.

These heroes have proven that 'adoption' is the new badge of honour. The adoption, not purchase, of dogs, is definitely the new Black.

Every single time I encounter an abandoned, neglected or abused dog; every moment I hear of irresponsible, unethical, unprofessional pet boarders; whenever I hear of human ego getting in the way of dog welfare; when my paths cross with cruel, nasty dog owners, it makes me want to hug my dog a little tighter and not let go.

Pets are forever. And forever doesn't mean "as long as it's convenient for you".

This book celebrates the wonderful people that have opened their hearts and their homes to these unfortunate canines, and the lives that have been enriched, both two- and four-legged. All their stories are different but the one thing that binds them all together is the love and empathy that all of them have extended to the less fortunate.

Every single one of these dogs is an inspiration to me. For their strength, their resilence, their unwavering and unconditional love. Every single one of the doggie owners has touched me with their selfless generousity, their big hearts and their patience and love.

I wish I had half the courage, dedication and drive that these fellow dog owners have. They are all inspirational in their own way, and motivate me each and every single day and spur me on to do better for my canine companion and to be a more responsible dog owner.

All of them have taught me lessons which has enabled me to be a better pawrent to Leia.
I am still learning every day.

> 66
> **There is something about a dog that you rescue from a shelter... there's an appreciation you'll never see from any other dog that understands that you rescued them, and it's the best feeling when you see those dogs come to life and change and all of a sudden blossom into what they're supposed to be. It's the best feeling so go rescue a dog if you can.**
> 99
>
> ELLEN DEGENERES

FOREWORD
#DoingBetterForMan'sBestFriend

"Mister, my house is not a Zoo. I cannot have animals running all over the place!"

This was the response I received when I asked someone why she kept her three dogs in cages in her home. The property was a large landed house, with a sizeable garden, and would have appeared to have been a great home for man's best friend. But all three Cavalier King Charles Spaniels were caged up for most of the day, only let out for very short durations. Each dog was bought for one of her three young children.

The practice of caging or chaining a dog is not uncommon in Singapore. There are many dogs out there who spend most, if not all, of their day confined and barely able to move. The reasons provided by these dogs owners have similar themes.

One of the most common is that someone in the household had bought the animal, very possibly without considering the significant commitment that comes with pet keeping, and then was unable or unwilling to appropriately manage the dog. To address the problem of the dog running out the gate, digging up the garden, destroying furniture and soiling the home, the animal is kept neatly tucked away in a cage or on a chain in a corner of the house. Problem solved.

Other common reasons provided are that someone in the home is allergic to or afraid of the animal or that a new baby is in the home. Confining the dog, which is simple and easy to do, is then seen as the most convenient way to deal with the situation.

And then there are the reasons associated with attitudes towards pet keeping. There were many a time when I, a young SPCA inspector, who turned up at someone's home to speak with them about their confined dog, was faced with absolute bewilderment by the dog's owner. I remember the countless faces looking at me in amusement, wondering why someone, in an official looking shirt and pants no less, would take the trouble to travel all the way to their home to speak about their caged or chained dog. I was soon faced with replies such as, "if dogs are not allowed in cages, why do pet shops sell them", "it's a dog, its meant to be chained up!" and "show me the law that says a dog cannot be caged".

Animals need to be able to perform natural behaviours and require sufficient space to do so. They also strongly prefer their toileting area be kept separate from the rest of their environment. A confined dog clearly cannot meet these needs. Keeping a dog confined for long periods can also be psychologically distressing for the animal. Social isolation, which is usually a consequence of long duration caging and chaining, compounds the problem. All things considered, this is a serious welfare issue.

As the reasons this unacceptable practice is carried out are varied, the solutions must be equally multi-pronged. Education and awareness is required for those who do not realise their actions are causing harm while strong enforcement action is required for the dog owners who refuse to provide their pets with a basic standard of living.

The team at SPCA and other kind spirited individuals have rescued many dogs from endless confinement, either by working with the dog owners to improve conditions for the animal or by taking the dog out of the situation and finding them better homes.

The issue of confinement is just one of many, that affects dogs in Singapore. Abuse, neglect and abandonment are some of the other miseries that a dog may suffer. But it is certainly not all doom and gloom. This book, and the beautiful stories within, gives much hope for the dogs out there waiting to be rescued.

Jaipal Singh Gill (Dr)
Executive Director
Society for the Prevention of Cruelty to Animals, (SPCA)
Singapore

PROLOGUE
#WhatIsThePerfectDog

What is the perfect dog?

Is it measured by their long glossy coats or by their show dog worthy aesthetics?

Some search for the purest breed; others for a common household name; some end up paying thousands of dollars for their perfect dog.

I paid 100 RMB for my perfect dog, a tri-colored female mongrel from a small clothing store along a roadside in Suzhou, China, 12 years ago. The storekeeper had a dog who just gave birth to a litter of puppies. She only accepted money for the puppy because she wanted to ensure that it would instill a sense of awareness and responsibility towards the dog. Dolly is not just my perfect dog, she is my world.

Dolly has brought so much joy to my family and I, joy that no amount of money can buy. I have fond memories of her sleeping by my bedside when I'm sick, kissing my face whenever I cry, and doing silly little things to make me laugh. She has given birth to two amazing little boys that are just as perfect as she is, and all three have helped me care for all the strays that I've brought home over the years.

My family and I have brought home puppies who were abandoned, mistreated, neglected or given up by their former owners. We have cared for dogs with canine parvovirus, nursed them back to health and given them a second shot at life with a brand new family.

Dolly, and her two boys Dally and Junior, have taught me that the genetic makeup and physical appearance of a dog does not define their perfection. I've seen puppies and grown dogs being cast aside because they don't come from a purebred family, that they have the "wrong" coat colour, or that they are too slow, too sick, or even old, to be a part of someone's family.

A dog is perfect to you because it loves and understands you, all of which it gives to you unconditionally. I learned that the only thing that matters when having a dog is to give it love and companionship, and that taught me how to love unconditionally as well. Having my own dogs also made me a better dog lover, because I was able to open my heart up to all the other dogs that I have been so fortunate to care for and to have found families that are willing to do the same for them as well.

There are so many dogs out there that need a family, dogs that can't be found in pet stores, dogs that have been through rough times. They are all perfect in their own little ways. And we are perfect to them. We are their everything, and that's all that really matters.

Cheryl Chou
Miss Universe Singapore 2016
Actress/Host

#ANewHope

I was at Voices For Animals one Saturday morning in October 2017 to meet a rescued Weimaraner named Meredith. There, I was introduced to the founder of the animal welfare group, a gentleman by the name of Derrick. As we chattered about rescues and ex-breeding dogs and the commitment required for Meredith, I realised that, perhaps, I wasn't the right fit for this particular animal.

"Hold on," he said. "I'll be right back," and disappeared around the corner. A split second later, he reappeared with the most gorgeous canine by his side, a deadringer for my late dog Hock. "This is Elia," her matchmaker introduced us. She took a few tentative steps into the room and made a beeline for me. There was an instant connection.

Elia, along with her breeding partner, were two of 180 dogs rescued from a Pasir Ris pet farm that was shut by the authorities in 2017. It was reported in local media that the owner of Top Breed Pet Farm, Edwin Tan Guowei was convicted of six of eleven charges, including his failure to treat eight dogs found in poor health during a surprise inspection by AVA, breach of farm licensing conditions and operating an unlicensed pet shop. He was sentenced on 7 June 2017, fined S$180,000 and disqualified from running any animal-related business for six months.

There was a certain sadness in her eyes, yet she was affectionate, loving and trusting. She was shy, pensive and a tad apprehensive but walked beautifully on the leash. She was also incredibly quiet. Not a bark, not a whine, not even a whimper. There was something about this dog that I couldn't quite explain, but I knew I had fallen under her spell.

Before I left, she leaned her head ever so gently against my thigh, and my heart skipped a beat. I turned to Derrick and said I'd adopt her.

But first, I had to sort out schedules and administrative matters. October and November were two of my busiest months in the year. I did not want to bring her home and not have time to spend with her. Derrick allowed me to leave her at the boarding house and pick her in December. I proceeded to prepare my house and my life to welcome her.

I spent the next two months researching everything about her breed, their habits, their idiosyncrasies, training, diet, lifestyle et al. I spent all my free time trawling the internet for suitable doggie products, and many other frivolous moments ordering an array of doggie accessories. I cleared out an area in my house as her space, and began construction on an extension at the back of the building, which would house her kitchen and dining area, as well as a side gate, so that she would have her own private garden 'to hang out' when I was at work. I visited Elia as often as I could.

 Each time we met, I learnt a little more about the girl. It has been a good two-and-a-half decades since Hock's demise, so I had to relearn everything about caring for canines. I stumbled upon

some fab YouTube sites with educational training tips and devoured them with a vengeance.

The two months zipped by like quicksilver and it was soon the night before I was due to pick her up. The house was all prepped to welcome its newest member. I had her bed positioned in the perfect corner of the house, strategically placed between the two Walter Van Beirendonck rugs in perfect shades of tangerine and scarlet – the best colours to compliment the colour of her fur! I had her colour-coordinated toys all laid out, her array of matching leashes and martingale collars hanging in on a wall, her mini-fridge filled with treats. I started an instagram account to document her journey with me and couldn't wait to fill it with her pictures.

Before I met Elia, I could not play with another dog without feeling like I was cheating on Hock. I felt so guilty each time I socialised with them. When I was living in Europe, I used to go on long evening walks with fashion designer Lezley George's adopted retired racing Greyhound, Lola, in London, and hung out with a male model's Goldie, Pascal, in Amsterdam. I wondered each time if Hock was looking down at us from the rainbow bridge and if he would approve.

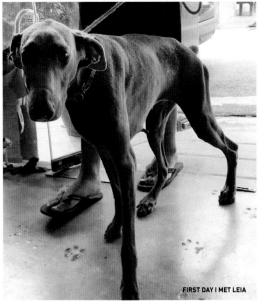

FIRST DAY I MET LEIA

I was so nervous and restless that Friday night. What would Hock think? Would I make a good pawrent? Would she love me? What if? What if?

That night, Hock appeared in my dreams. It was almost as if he was giving his approval, telling me to "love her like you loved me, and much much more".

I showed up at Sunny Heights the next day, a tad sleepy but emotionally settled, knowing I had Hock's approval. I think she was as nervous as I, resting her head tentatively on my lap throughout the ride home. I enlisted the help of Fred, a rewards-based trainer to help her assimilate into the household. He was waiting at my home as part of her welcome party to ensure her first impression of the house was as stress-free as possible. She commemorated the occasion with a welcome poo in the garden, which we celebrated with much gusto and treats! She soon caught on and realised grass is for peeing and pooing! Toilet training after was a breeze.

I renamed her Leia, after the princess in *Star Wars*, and, like royalty, she swept through the house, claiming her spots and ignoring all the spaces I had painstakingly chosen for her. She completely disregarded the fluffy bed and lay down instead on the orange 'tiger' rug. She did not know what to make of the toys and avoided them. She seemed to prefer the hard concrete floor of the back porch to the comfort of her bed. Hard cold floors are probably all she's known her whole life. "Be patient," I told myself.

I never heard a sound from her. She communicated through her large expressive eyes. I was beginning to wonder if she had been debarked.

I brought her to the vet a couple of days later for a full medical checkup. I was more concerned about her pronounced limp, which I wanted to address immediately. In my research on ex-breeding dogs, I realised that many of them come with hip and hind limb issues, due to the trauma they were subjected to in the mill. I could tell she was in pain, both mentally and physically. It was absolutely heart-rending. Her vet informed me that her ligaments were stressed, the result (I'm assuming) of imprisonment in cages too small for her.

This piece of news hit me like a ton of bricks. She was in urgent need of surgery. Dr Nic ran through all the options with me and gave me his recommendations. The most effective was TPLO, or tibial-plateau-leveling osteotomy, a surgery performed on dogs to stabilize the stifle joint after ruptures of the cranial cruciate ligament. It was also the most expensive procedure but the best one for Leia if I wanted to give her some semblance of a good life. I needed to find the money somehow but I only had one ass to sell. I gave the green light nonetheless, and she went under the knife barely three weeks after her adoption.

I was worried, distressed and upset. Worried that our bond might be irrevocably damaged because she might now associate her new home with pain, inconvenience and the Elizabethan collar; distressed because I wasn't sure if I was doing enough for her,

or proficient enough to take on the role as her caregiver and nurse her back to health.

I also got spectacularly trolled immediately after the surgery – ironically, by the same person who introduced me to the idea of adoption. I was chastised for being a bad dog owner, lambasted for causing her pain and reproached for her confusion and distress. I was accused on her Facebook page of adopting for my own publicity. 'A dog is for life', she stated the obvious, giving me a lecture on caring for shelter dogs whilst cradling her own pet-shop-bought designer canine in her delicate, manicured arms.

One of the most educational things I took away from being on *Asia's Next Top Model* is how to deal with trolls, so I promptly ignored her, and plunged headlong into giving my dog the best life I can possibly accord.

Leia has metal rods inserted in her left and right hind legs. The surgeries were done ten months apart from each other. She is also undergoing hydrotherapy to strengthen the muscles in her legs. I have to monitor her movements and limit her activities for a year whilst her leg heals.

Leia is small for her breed. I guess proper nutrition isn't priority at a mill that is driven by profit. She was skin and bones when I first saw her, and I had to fight the temptation to overcompensate on her meals. I need to maintain her weight to avoid placing undue stress on her injured legs. It saddens me to have to stop her from enthusiastically running around with wild abandon or initiating play with other dogs, but I need to let her heal completely or risk further injury.

When I decided to adopt her, I started to research unethical breeders and puppy mills extensively but had to stop as it was too horrifying. Scenes of the terrible conditions of her past life kept replaying in my head over and over again. Female dogs have it worst. They are impregnated by the male dogs the minute they have their first heat cycle, and subsequently at every successive cycle. All the owners care about is to milk as many puppies as possible from the mothers. It's almost like

doggie rape. When the puppies are born, they are taken away from their mothers before they are properly weaned. It must have been absolutely traumatic for her and the other breeding dogs.

Leia is an intelligent and highly sensitive dog. She is shy but curious, wary but inquisitive. She is quietly pensive, always deep in thought. I sometimes wonder what she is thinking, and the idea of approaching an animal communicator has crossed my mind several times. After I adopted her, I realised that we are alike in so many ways. We both have ligament issues – her first operation was on her left hind leg and I have a torn PCL on my same leg! We suffer from skin allergies and break out in the occasional rash. We are even prescribed almost the same meds from our respective docs! Like me, she has sinus. We both snore, and always inadvertently end up with a dripping nose and sneezing fits each time we sleep in air conditioned comfort. Its amazing how we both mirror each other's health issues.

We share the same dramatic streak too. She welcomed Chinese New Year 2018 spectacularly with the onset of her heat cycle. I woke that morning to puddles of red blood all over the house. She looked up and grinned as I ran around the house screaming, almost as if to say "Welcome to the Year of the Dog!"

After more than a year, she has settled very well into the house. She loves sleeping on her beds and gets an immense thrill out of a boisterious game of tug of war with her squeaky toys. Her personality has started to shine through. She has finally found her voice, and would not hesitate to sound

a warning bark to defend her home. She has also become more physically fit and muscular, thanks to her therapy and daily exercise.

I have had to make several changes to my life now that I have a dog. I walk her religiously every morning and night so that she would get her exercise. No more sleeping in or putting the alarm on perpetual snooze! When I have early call times, I wake even earlier so I can spend quality time with her – 6am call times mean 4am walks and 5am meals. Late night schedules result in 1am walks. There are not many dog-friendly establishments so I don't dine out as often as I used to. Instead, I order in, and have occasional picnics with her in the garden instead. She enjoys her car rides, and we constantly break out into carpool karaoke every time *Bohemian Rhapsody* or any Abba song comes on! I sing to her in the shower and talk to her constantly. I have also grown a thick skin and grown oblivious to the incredulous stares from people who think I've gone off my rockers for carrying on a conversation with my dog!

That thick skin has also help me deal with the critics. I've been accused of spending too much money on her, and also for not spending enough money. For spending too much time with her, and for not spending enough time. For loving her too much or not loving her enough. I am guilty of all of the above crimes. I spend a shitload of money on her, yet it doesn't seem to be enough. I spend a lot of time with her but feel guilty each time I leave the house, even if it's for a grocery run.

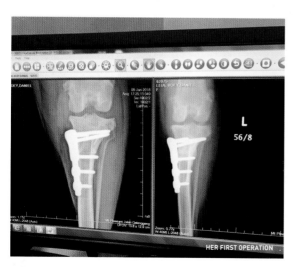

HER FIRST OPERATION

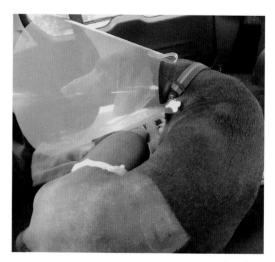

I try to give her as good a life as I can possible afford, but wonder if that is more that I can do. Part of it stems from the guilt I carry for not having done all I could for Hock when he was alive.

I've been criticised for wasting so much money on her operation, on hydrotherapy and even on training! Guilty! Guilty! Guilty! Yes, they're really expensive but absolutely necessary. I've had to make adjustments to my own life, and cut back on my own expenditure in order to afford it. I've become more selective when buying clothes. I am more strategic when purchasing accessories. And do I really need new bags and shoes every season?

I am just so blown away by how close knit and how incredibly supportive the international doggie community is. When I posted pictures of Leia's surgical procedures on Instagram and Facebook, I was inundated with not just get-well wishes but links and websites sent by vets and owners the world over whose dogs had undergone the same procedure. We have become a global support system: sharing advice, exchanging notes and bolstering spirits. Through this network, I learnt about Harrasburg Horns and Grafmar's Caps, which gave me a clue to the origins of my dog's ancestry.

Leia has brought so much joy into my life, and I have such a strong reason to live. Before her, I had a *laissez-faire* attitude to life. If I'm meant to go, then I'll go quietly into the night. Today, I have a life that is depending on me for her survival, so I keep myself fighting fit so that I can stay alive to care for her. My life is her life and vice versa. As much as I want her to live forever, I hope she will go before I do. I've read too many horror stories of dogs who end up in limbo, surrendered to the authorities to be put down or abandoned and left to their own devices when their owners pass that I dread to think of where she might end up or the kind of life she might be subjected to should I depart before her.

Makeup artiste Dollei Seah commented that I smile a lot more these days, and I now walk with a bounce in my step. I've become less angsty and more selective with my time and the people I hang out with. Whenever I'm faced with a situation, I ask myself WWLD (What Would Leia Do?). And it helps me tackle the problem head-on with a lot more patience, honesty and understanding. I also roll my eyes a lot less often! My dog is the role model by which I set the standard for the values and types of people I want in my circle. I now prefer to surround myself with happy, positive people who build each other up.

I am committed to giving Leia the best life that I can possible accord her. Every day with her is a joy; every single waking moment spent in her company is time to be treasured. We do our best as pawrents to help them adapt to life in our world. I have an added responsibility – to help her forget as much of her past as possible.

I know that we are both not alone in this journey. I can still feel Hock's presence and I know he is guiding and protecting Leia as she learns how to be a dog again.

LEIA PICKS OUT DESIGNER RUGS

LEIA CLAIMS HER RUGS

#IKnow
I'llNeverLove
ThisWayAgain

'You know my friend has Buddy, right? Leia's ex-lover. He has a wonderful forever home now. Best people ever, and even a new girlfriend.'

I received that text message from my former agent one day in August, seven months after I adopted Leia. We were discussing outfits for the premiere of *Crazy Rich Asians* when the conversation suddenly segued into our rescue dogs. Which led to the discussion of Leia's old flame.

My first encounter with Buddy was through a photograph sent to me by the shelter. He was then known as Loras, and his matchmaker had asked if I would like to consider adopting both Leia and Loras. I could only handle one dog, so I took Leia and left a heartbroken Loras behind. I promised Loras I would touch base with him once he had been adopted and we would arrange playdates with both dogs.

Through sheer coincidence and three degrees of separation, Loras' new pawrent was a good friend of my former agent. She adopted the handsome boy one month after I took Leia home.

"In January 2018, my 5-year-old son Callum and I decided we were ready to adopt a 'Callum' dog. We went to an adoption drive organised by a local shelter, and shortlisted a few medium sized dogs that might have been suitable for him. However, the founder of the animal welfare group saw Marci, our other dog, and asked if we would like to consider Loras. We were excited and said yes, but with several caveats. We needed to see if Marci liked him and if both dogs could get along. He had to get the approval of my helper Julie, who is the person who does most of the feeding and cleaning. I had to assess his temperament and see if he could fit into the family dynamics. He had to like Callum, and vice-versa."

We popped to the shelter the next day and Loras was introduced to us.

"I saw a tired looking dog with half-opened eyes, droopy eye lids, swinging long nipples, underweight, scarred, with huge paws that were disproportionate to his body.

Through the shelter, we found out that Buddy was rescued from a breeding farm, together with his breeding partner, Leia. They were under nourished, under weight, unloved, confined in a cage too small for them. Forced to breed to fatten the breeder's wallet. Buddy was clueless, nervous, fearful yet yearned for a companion, which he found in Leia. But flip the coin, and you find Leia, on the other hand, confident, strong, with a strong mind of her own who just wanted to be left alone when faced with Buddy. Imagine a loveless arranged marriage and used as a breeding machine. Nasty!"*

BUDDY

I knew all about this infamous case. I remember reading that the fine imposed on the breeder was "the highest imposed on anyone for committing animal cruelty and welfare-related offences."

However, regardless of how high the fine was, no amount of punishment would be fair compensation for the horrific life he inflicted upon the hapless dogs, nor the trauma they experienced. Humans could simply pay the fine, serve their jail term and resume their life again, but for the animals, many of them become emotionally and physically scarred for life, with some of them paying for the cruelty of the breeders with their lives.

"Buddy had been kept in a cage with his breeding partner. From what we gathered, they were probably kept in a small cage. Both dogs did not sign up to be parents but were forced to breed. I can't begin to image their frustrations, their fear and their uncertainties, not to mention their discomfort and the trauma of living in inhumane conditions.

Buddy's paw pads were not properly developed and he had two dangling 3-inch long nipples. He was a sad, malnourished 21 kg when he was rescued from the mill.

It was heart breaking to see a beautiful boy reduced to such sorry state due to the greed and vanity of humans."

Buddy was scared, shy, a little confused and completely disinterested in us. He did, however, show a slight tweak of curiousity towards Marci.

Marci, on the other hand, was estatic! She kept wanting to play with him. *"I have not seen her this excited since my late dog, the 11-year-old Boris, died suddenly in his sleep four months prior. Julie and I were shocked at the condition of this dog, and our hearts went out to him. We tried to engage him but he was totally disinterested in us.*

I knew, however, that I wanted to adopt this boy and help him get better. But I promised my husband James that I would be rational and not make any rash, impulse decisions."

Eva arranged for a follow up visit, this time with Callum. *"I was shocked at how well they both got along. Loras responded so well to my young son, walked well on leash with him and was most gentle. However, he still refused to interact with me!"*

By then, Eva was totally convinced she wanted to take him home. He had the approval of Marci and Callum, and she was sure, with lots of love and care, that he would warm up to her eventually.

"I arranged for a third visit. Marci was dropped off at doggie day care, where she would spend the day mingling and playing with Loras. It also gave me the chance to assess if there was any potential aggression from either dog. That evening, we arranged for Loras to accompany Marci home in the doggie bus.

We stayed behind to complete the paperwork and pay the adoption fee. His minders were happy, but I could sense a smidgen of concern. They were overjoyed that Loras had found a home but were also worried that he would fail the home trial."

Eva and the family plunged straight into helping him through his first night, but not before giving him a new name. They decided to call him Buddy.

"It was really a process of trial and error. I have grown up around dogs and had my first when I was 11. However, this was our first rescue and we had no idea what was going through his mind nor how to help him overcome his fears. He had no idea what was happening or where he was. Till now, he had only the experience of living in the hell hole known as the puppy mill and his few short months at the shelter, so the concept of a home was completely new and foreign to him. He paced up and down the house for four hours straight, stopping only to pee and poo.

The first three nights were as difficult for us as it was for him, but we stayed by his side.

He was a nervous wreck. He did not stop whining and barking, and carried on for the better part of the night. I stayed with him, keeping him company on the ground floor. He refused flatly to join me in my room on the third floor and would not touch the sofa on the second floor. He had no idea how to get

comfortable. He was uneasy with how quiet the house was at night, did not touch his bed and treated the entire house like a toilet. He was totally unsure of what was going on around him"

Still, the family persevered.

Eva and Julie did not sleep a wink those first few nights.

It was Marci who helped Buddy settle in and he gradually began to relax.

"We tried to spend as much time with Buddy as possible and show him as much love as he would allow. We also tried to create a calm, safe, loving environment within the house. We were determined not to fail him."

Fortunately for them, Buddy had no aggression issues. But it got tricky, health-wise. Buddy had tick fever, so they had to medicate not just him but Marci also. The minute he got better, they decided to send him for a quick nip/tuck. Buddy was already neutered, so the procedure of getting his saggy nipples removed was fairly uncomplicated. His teeth were in a terrible condition so Eva had them scaled too.

As for his skin condition, he was under observation for suspected lupus. Good news came several months later – it wasn't lupus but a severe allergy. He is now on lifetime medication, which he has to ingest every alternate day, a slow and laborious process but thankfully, there has been visible improvement.

"Buddy is like a large teddy bear. He loves being hugged and babied by everyone in the family. He is also a very casual dog. He will casually check out the dining table for food. He will casually step up to my bed for a hug. And he will casually saunter up to the vet during consultation.

"Marci and Buddy have become best friends, and he has warmed up to Julie and Eva. But he is especially protective of Callum. It's almost as if he knew Callum was heartbroken after the death of Boris, and tried to comfort him.

"Boris was the kindest soul and well loved by everyone. I had 11 wonderful years with him. He saw me through my divorce, my moves, my miscarriages, shared my happiness, my son, my husband and my bed. He never left my side and was like my guardian angel. He protected me physically and emotionally. I see a lot of Boris in Buddy. He has taken it upon himself to protect Callum, Marci and his new found family

it is hugely rewarding to see Buddy slowly blossoming into a dorky, silly, happy boy who loves his daily zoomies, galavanting with his park friends and behaving like a puppy. Seeing those sad eyes slowly opening up to their full, curious, naughty mode, and the smiles that he has nowadays. He is growing into exactly the role he is meant to fulfil in our house – a happy, henpecked, "lala" boy who sees Callum, our son, as his protector, and vice-versa."

> ❝
> ## Love them for one second and they will love you for eternity.
> ❞

EVA WONG

BUDDY AND LEIA AND THE MAN WHO RESCUED THEM

#PleaseDon't LetMeBe Misunderstood

"OMG!!!!"

Terry was breathless with excitement, almost choking over his café latte as he struggled to get all his words out at once.

"I just photographed the most beautiful Dobie!!!!!! You MUST meet him. He is GORGEOUS!!!!!"

Terry Peh and I were having tea at a Joo Chiat coffee house one afternoon. He was recounting his experience shooting the shelter alumni for their annual calendar when we suddenly had a brainwave.

"Why don't you put rescue dogs on the runway and show the world how beautiful they all are?" I said. "I can speak to Addie, the owner of NOW model management, who used to show dogs in his younger days, to support you. And rope in the many dog-loving Singapore designers to create merchandise for GoodDogPeople? Oh, and put Uno in the show too!!!" I managed to slip that in at the end of the conversation.

I have always had an affinity for Dobermans ever since I had Ah Hock in the nineteen eighties. It is a handsome breed of comparatively modern origin, having surfaced only towards the end of the nineteenth century, the result of mixing several dog breeds, including the German Shepherd, the Weimaraner, Rottweiler, Great Dane and Terrier. Dobermans were bred in Germany initially as protectors but have evolved into excellent family dogs. They are kind, playful, loving, loyal, beautiful, affectionate, athletic and sleek and intensely loyal. They are also, along with Pit Bulls, Rottweilers and several other breeds, one of the most misunderstood dogs.

I could not wait to meet Uno and counted the days impatiently till the fashion show. I wondered if he would be anything like Hock? If he would like me? If he and Leia would get along? Would he would behave at the show? Would I like his owners?

UNO I assigned a model with much experience in handling big dogs as his modelling partner. Male model Derrick Lee, the owner of the Belgian Malinois-lookalike Singapore Special Maya, was as excited as I to meet him. He did not disappoint. Uno is even more stunning in real life than in pictures. He has the most soulful eyes that pierce straight into the depths of your soul; he's got a wonderful temperament and the gentlest demeneour. Even Leia was enamoured by him. I wondered how a beautiful dog like him could've ended up in the shelter.

"Uno was probably bred by a backyard breeder and born in November 2011. He was purchased by his previous owner, possibly as a guard dog for his fish farm at Choa Chua Kang, and named Hilton. That was where he spent his formative years."

Hilton probably grew up amongst the workers and possibly had the company of other mixed-breed dogs which used to frequent the area. I can just imagine the sort of devil-may-care, happy-go-lucky life he must have led, running around the farm with wild abandon and not a care in the world, chasing the cats and squirrels that inhabited the vicinity of Choa Chu Kang, running after motorcycles, barking at intruders and protecting his owners. What a glorious world to grow up in. That probably explains why he is so wonderfully socialised with humans and remains calm in their company. It's probably one of the reasons why he got along so well with Leia too. They probably spent all that time backstage discussing the best ways to catch felines, rodents and other scurrying creatures.

When the owner lost his business, he was unfortunately unable to take Hilton with him as he lived in an HDB flat, where such breeds were not permitted. It must have been so upsetting for him to have to make that decision to give his beloved companion up.

He approached ASD, a local shelter, to assist with his rehoming. Meanwhile, Hilton was placed at a boarding kennel right next to ASD, where he stayed whilst waiting for his forever home to materialise.

"To his last owner's credit, and, I'd like to think, commitment or love, he'd spent his own money to pay for the boarding without abandoning him. That boarding would have cost him thousands."

Hilton spent close to three long years at the kennel. It was a drastic change from the carefree life he came to enjoy at the farm. He had about 20 minutes a day to run around but was otherwise locked up in his kennel.

After three years, even his kennel handlers were keen to see him rehomed. It was almost like he had served three years (or half his life) in prison. To put it in human perspective, he was incarcerated at age 21 (through no fault of his own) with an opportunity for parole only at age 49!

Hilton was close to a volunteer named Sue, who walked him once a week whenever she came by. She was anxious to see him re-homed or fostered out as soon as possible, as she was moving back to Australia.

Being fostered would give him a chance to live in a family environment for at least part of his life.

"I first saw Hilton in an online ad for rehoming dogs which incorrectly described him as mixed-breed. From my experience, I knew from the photo that he was a Doberman. So I got in touch with ASD to find out more about him."

Kelvin lost Boris, his Doberman of almost 13 years when he passed away on Valentine's Day in 2017. Although he decided against having another dog, the house felt strangely quiet, especially when he was used to living in a home with dogs for almost 30 years.

So he made the decision to foster, which would allow him the freedom of not committing to a dog for a lifetime, especially in view of his travel commitments.

He decided to specifically foster Cat B dogs. These are breeds that are the hardest to rehome, as owners are faced with a plethora of rules, regulations and policies imposed by AVA. These conditions discourage the majority of Singaporeans from adopting them, resulting in the dogs spending a longer time in the shelter.

Dobermans, together with German Shepherds, Pitbulls, Bull Terriers and Rottweilers, are Cat B dogs. They are labelled so because they are deemed aggressive. One look at Hilton and you know he is far from so. Dobermans are fiercely loyal, yet they have the sweetest souls. Some dobies are even afraid of their own shadow!

"

Getting to know your dog is like learning a new foreign language. You learn about their physiology and psychology. You need to spend the time to interact with them like living, breathing beings, and not treat them as part of the furniture, or spoil them! You also need lots of commitment. If most people won't abandon their children, why would you abandon your dog?

"

KELVIN AND NANCY

"I decided to give first preference to Dobermans and Rottweilers, as I have 15 years of experience dealing with Dobermans. I have built up the right infrastructure at home, my family members are familiar with the breed and I have a trainer who worked with me to train my two (late) Dobermans. It would also be a great opportunity to give one of these misunderstood dogs a second chance at life."

Kelvin's discussion with ASD centered around fostering till they could find him a home. The shelter was a tad reluctant but decided in favour of the foster as there were no realistic prospects of finding a new home in the near future.

Hilton began his homestay almost immediately, and went ballistic in his new surroundings. He was like a prisoner who had just been released after a long sentence. He spent his days running up and down the fence chasing cars and motorcycles and barked at everyone.

Kelvin and Nancy decided to rename him Uno.

"I was not sure what to expect after not having had a new dog for more than 10 years. My family members were all excited and curious to see him when he arrived.

He had no concept of toilet habits, and had to be retrained from scratch. In the first week, we would wake up to a back kitchen wet from his pee.

Family members were terribly frustrated as everyone was used to well trained and disciplined dogs. Our previous dogs had become so familiar, I could grunt and they would know what I wanted. If I told them to sit in one spot, they would do so, sometimes for over an hour because I forgot to release them!!!"

Because of his age and past experience, Kelvin knew he had to take a different approach with Uno, starting with a lowering of expectations. He knew it would be unfair to compare him with his previous dogs, who started their training as puppies

He began by giving him a new sense of routine, and started him on basic obedience training.

There was some progress after two months, as he learnt the norms of living in this household.

"It really brought home to me the challenges of adopting a middle-aged or older dog. It can be much harder to socialise him into the household compared to a puppy, but it is not impossible. You have to work with what you have, because it is not so easy to teach new habits.

I remember the first time we bought him a Coolaroo elevated pet bed. It is his absolute favourite thing in the world. After sleeping on bare concrete most of his life, it is a luxury he now deserves."

After fostering him for two months, Kelvin and Nancy decided to adopt him.

"He had grown accustomed to living with us, and us with him. Life actually gained a certain sense of familiarity with him in the house. My first dobie

Storm passed on prematurely at the age eight on Christmas Day 2011. Uno is almost like a reincarnation of her, except for the fact that he was born a month before she died.

They both share so many similar characteristics. He is smart and wilful, just like her. They even sit in a similar fashion."

Uno is Kelvin's third Doberman, and his sixth dog. He's had a Lab-mix and a Silky Terrier and also fostered his sister's West Highland White Terrier, apart from the two Dobermans. He was, however, closest to the two dobies. The relationship was established through a regular regime of training and exercise, which allowed them to build the bond.

"I'm a firm believer in regular training, as it helps both you and your dog understand each other and grow closer.

With my previous Dobermans, we spent at least two to three hours a day on walks and obedience training – first thing in the morning, after work and sometimes late into the night.

When you are really close to your dog, you can communicate with them purely by looking at each other. I had that with Boris. With Storm, who passed on before Boris, she understood language to the point I could even make requests – not issue commands –and she would know what to do.

I have not reached that stage with Uno and perhaps I never will. I haven't had the time to build those bonds with him.

He is not as disciplined as I am used to, but I accept it. It is hard to train an older dog, and it requires more commitment to training than I have at this stage of my life.

It doesn't help that his favourite motivator in the world is not food or walks but sleep! How do you train a dog whose favourite activity is sleeping? He has been known to get up in the morning for breakfast, and then go back to bed.

We were very lucky that he was well socialised and well loved growing up on the farm. We have had no major behavioural issues to deal with. He has integrated well with the family and makes a very good companion for my father when I am travelling.

Uno is a quick learner, and is a very clever, thinking dog.

"When he first came, he realised he could slip out of his collar if he was in the right position. You could still see him occasionally trying to slip out, as if it is a game. It's a sign of intelligence.

He also has very expressive and intelligent eyes. He will always look you in the eye and try to read your mind. You can almost see the train of thought passing through his mind."

If you look into a Dobie's eyes, you will see an honest and loving soul.

Dobermans like Uno are often called velcro dogs because they grow very attached to their owners and simply attach themselves to them! They will follow them everywhere! They also have very kind hearts.

Most dogs like Uno are not aggressive by nature. When they are, it is either through provocation, reaction to a perceived threat, abuse or because they were trained to do so. Even a Chihuahua would bite, if provoked. When they growl, it is a calming signal to stay away. Most dogs would rather avoid conflict than to start it. Unfortunately, most dog conflicts are started by humans, and the dogs are the unfortunate ones who pay the price.

Dogs like Uno are greatly misunderstood. If more dog owners took the time to research their dog behaviour and invest time and effort in training them, learning how to handle and communicate with, and building a bond with their dogs, like Kelvin has done, there would be no need for mass hysteria and Category B.

"

Saving one dog will not change the world, but surely for that one dog, the world will change forever.

"

KAREN DAVIDSON
AUTHOR
"A DOG'S GUIDE TO HUMANS"

SHOT ON LOCATION
@
CAPELLA SINGAPORE

"
You can't change a dog's past,
but you could REWRITE his future.
"

“
Dogs are not our whole life, but they make our lives whole.

”

ROGER CARAS

"

Folk will know how large your soul is,
by the way you treat a dog.

"

CHARLES F. DORAN

#YearOfTheDog

"More Canines Given Up After 2006's Year Of The Dog" screamed the headline of a local newspaper on the 12 February 2018.

According to the Executive Director of the SPCA Dr Jaipal Singh Gill, there is usually a spike in the purchase of dogs when their Chinese zodiac sign rolls around. Many of these are impulse buys, only to be abandoned when the novelty wears off. Shortly after 2006's Year of the Dog, SPCA took in a total of 2,727 dogs, a significantly higher number, 518 of which were suspected to be abandoned.

It takes a very special breed of heartlessness and insensitivity to be able to throw an innocent, defenceless living creature who only has love and loyalty to their family out on the streets. Especially when it's done in the name of decluttering for good luck.

Do these people actually think they are getting good karma by throwing them out as part of spring cleaning for an auspicious festival? How auspicious can it be to indulge in such a hard-hearted, cruel, merciless act under the misguided veil of luck.

Thankfully, as much as there are cold-hearted beasts, there are also other compassionate, kind, generous souls out there who serve as the saviours and guardian angels to these unfortunate canines.

The Wang family have always opened their hearts and their houses to all manner of two- and four-legged creatures, humans included. They are generous to a fault, just to their friends but to all animals in need. From Singapore to Hong Kong to the US of A, we are always hearing these wonderful stories of the great rescue work the various members of the Wang clan, scattered around the world, are doing.

CELESTE
TIMBER
CHARCOAL

> 66
>
> **One of the most important lessons that I have learnt when adopting a dog is, if you are not willing to pay or if you are adopting because it is a cheaper alternative to buying, then please don't adopt because you would be doing it for all the wrong reasons. Having a dog is expensive and if you have no means of providing for them, then do not have a dog.**
>
> 99

MICHAEL WANG

"I've always grown up with dogs. My first was a rescued Poodle named Muffin who lived to the ripe old age of 18. My parents did not have her spayed and she went out one evening and came back pregnant. She produced a litter of beautiful puppies; we kept three of the litter and the rest were adopted. Keeping with the tradition, we named them after snacks, Sausage, Brownie and Cookie. By this point, we had also bought a Border Collie, which we named Sneakers, from a pet store, so we had a house with as many dogs as we had family members. For a child, it was a dream come true.

Sausage, Cookie and Brownie passed away tragically from eating a bad batch of food from a reputed dog food company. It was the first time I can recall having to come to terms with the death of a loved one. Anyone who has had a relationship with a dog knows the trauma and inexplicable pain of putting a dog to sleep. Muffin passed on some years later, followed by Sneakers. Each time, it really tore at me and I questioned whether I would ever be ready to be a dog owner again.

I went away for my studies, came back a few years later, got married and had kids of my own. When my children turned five and six, one of them brought up the prospect of keeping a dog. I knew it was just a purely impulsive request but it did force me to think about my own position on being a dog owner again, and whether I was ready for it. I muddled over it for a few months and decided that I was. I wanted the same kind of joy that my dogs of the past had brought me, growing up, so I broached the subject with my wife and she agreed.

My younger sister has an adopted dog, Lucky, a Singapore Special, adopted in 2006, I decided that I should follow in her stead and made an appointment to visit the shelter.

We had a very clear idea of the kind of dog we wanted. It had to be young, so that it could grow up with our children; the more puppy-like the better. We weaved our way in and out of the different cages, guided by the extremely professional dog ambassador and we saw a few dogs that were all about a few

CELESTE

years old. My children fell in love with a puppy named Peanut, but of course, it had already been adopted. All the dogs we saw were beautiful but I did not feel a bond with any of them. Wife and kids aside, I knew that the responsibility for choosing the dog lay with me since it was my decision to have the dog and it would be my responsibility to take care of it. The ambassador showed us the dogs that fit our brief. As we made our way through the shelter, a dog caught my eye. She was black with a bit of a brown on her chest, and she sat in her pen, and watched me with eyes that were kind and pleading at the same time.

'What about that one?'

The ambassador shuffled us over to the pen and we read the information on the dog. I was slightly disappointed to learn that she was eight years old. The ambassador asked if we would like to enter the pen to interact with Celeste and we did. I would not say that it was love at first sight, or that Celeste showed a remarkable connection with my children, but she seemed to be pretty excited when we took her out for a walk and she was by no means aggressive to my children. We returned

CHARCOAL

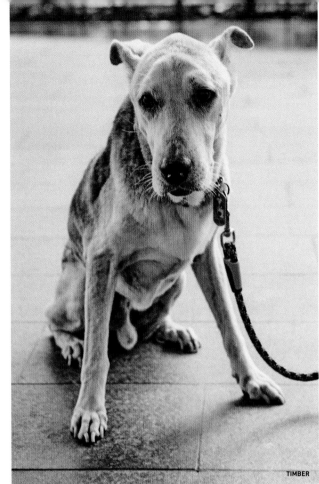

TIMBER

Celeste and saw a few more dogs that day. At night, when my kids were asleep, I had the talk with my wife about which dog we should adopt. My wife knew me well enough to know that I had already made up my mind and I informed the shelter that we would adopt Celeste."

Celeste was abandoned on the second day of Chinese New Year in 2009. She was tied to the railing of a pavilion in Clementi. Her leash was so short that she could not lie on the floor. She was about six to seven months old then. Next to her was a blanket, her toys and towels and a bowl of water. She was probably thrown out as part of a spring cleaning process. One cannot start to imagine how terrified, bewildered and unloved the young pup must have felt. She was rescued by Ricky, the founder of ASD, who remembers her as a very active dog. There were a few interested parties over the years but no takers, and she gradually grew old in the shelter. Eight years later,

in 2016, she made her way to Michael. She made the journey from her shelter in Lim Chu Kang to her new home and a brand new life.

There is always the apprehension of introducing a dog to new surroundings, but when Celeste came to our home, she bounded in, made a beeline for me and kept licking and licking my face. It was an unbridled joy of a dog who had been forgotten for so many years and was now the centre of attention. She was home.

There were the initial difficulties with Celeste which any owner has to overcome. In the first few days, she regarded anybody who was too close to me as a threat so she growled at my wife and children. But with time and patience, she learnt her place in the family and treated them with the same care and love as she treated me. It does take time to train a dog and all owners must be willing to put in the time to teach their dogs proper behaviour. Celeste continues to have anxiety issues when people she does not recognise visits the house; she barks when the doorbell is rung and when the visitor enters the house, she finds her own corner and eyeballs them. She has her odd quirks of accepting

55

Getting a dog is a lifetime of commitment and responsibility. It is not a passing fad to be discarded when the novelty and cuteness wears off and the realities of looking after a dog sets in.

RICKY YEO
ASD PRESIDENT

a person; those with long hair would find it easier to gain acceptance because she has a hair fetish. If a visitor sits on the floor with her hair down, Celeste would approach the visitor from the back and bury her head into the visitor's hair; soon after, she would accept you and would display no animosity should you try to touch her. She is not the kind of dog you can approach with an outstretched arm. At the end of the day, a dog is not a human being and should not be treated like one. A dog must be regarded as an individual being with moods and tantrums and quirks. Having the patience to know and understand this is important in building a relationship.

A few month after I adopted Celeste, my folks and I heard about another dog who had been at the shelter for eight years too. Apparently this dog was a favourite with all the volunteers so we were eager to meet him. My initial meeting with Timber one Saturday afternoon was underwhelming; I did not even get the chance to touch him. He was the complete opposite of Celeste; while Celeste regarded human presence with interest, Timber was a dog who shied away from any contact with human beings. He was very timid. My experience with Celeste taught me that I could make it work and we adopted Timber with the intention of having him placed as a companion for my younger sister's dog, Lucky.

When we first brought Timber to my parent's place, Timber did not like the space that he had. Such was his fear of everything that he found more comfort being in a small enclosed area. For six hours he buried himself in the soil in the corner of the garden and refused to move. By this point, it was about ten at night and I had to return home, so I decided that I would bring him back with me for the night.

Timber seemed to enjoy the stroll to my place and walked well on the leash. Timber and Celeste got along well. They could not care less for each other and hence were not aggressive in any way towards each other. Timber found comfort in the confined area of a storeroom and made his home there. It was apparent, at that point, that Timber would do better with me at my house than he would at my parent's place, and thus, he spends most of his time with us instead.

Timber has since overcome some of his fears; he no longer sleeps in the storeroom, unless it is raining (he hates thunder.) But a lot of fears still remains. He is the gentle giant; the kind of touch dog that you bring on a road show to let children play with. He is well-built and my wife enjoys taking him out for runs in the park; Celeste is unable to run well because her hind legs aren't strong. He did start to have skin problems when we adopted him, which was odd because he never had any problems at the shelter. Within a few months of his adoption, he started losing a lot of fur. We did an allergy test for him. It turns out he was allergic to a lot of different kinds of food and material — tomatoes, yeast, lamb, venison, cotton. It took a really long time to find the best food for him that was reasonably priced, and today, he has the most wonderful sheen to his coat.

My children spent a year with Timber and Celeste and grew to love them. It was everything I had hoped for, and brought back fond memories of my own childhood. Both dogs were so obedient that we decided to up the ante and adopted a puppy!

In 2017, my daughter asked if we could adopt another dog and this time, she requested that it be a puppy. I contacted Wendy from ASD and told them of my interest. By coincidence, they had just rescued two puppies from Tuas. Wendy brought Charcoal to see us in July of 2017, just in time for my daughter's birthday. Charcoal was four months when we adopted him. Having Charcoal was a real challenge because he was a puppy and with that comes the chewing and the scratching

CELESTE ABANDONED AT CLEMENTI

and the training. He seemed to have separation anxiety; whenever we left him at home for a few hours, he would tear the place to shreds. Even until today, he cannot be left in a house with a trash bin, even if it is covered, because he will topple it and happily spread your trash indiscriminately around the house. His favourite, to our horror, used to be the toilet brush; we once returned home to see him on our couch, chewing on our toilet brush. Thankfully, he has grown out of that.

Charcoal came to us puppy-size; he was small enough to go under Celeste's legs, much to her chagrin. He used to irritate Celeste by biting her tail until Celeste would snap at her. Within a matter of months, Charcoal was as big as Celeste and a few more months after, he was as big as Timber. Today, Charcoal is the biggest of all the family dogs, including Lucky. He continues to be the most difficult to manage. He does not approach dogs well; so eager is he to play that he lunges at them, which is often misconstrued by humans as aggression. He enjoys chasing dogs at dog parks too, which can be a problem for some other dog owners. I always have to be close enough to pull him back if he goes overboard.

The training never ends, and we continue to work on the dogs each time we bring them out. Charcoal, especially, is still overly excited but through time and patience and a methodical approach to teaching him, he no longer tears the house up. He has always been close to Celeste and she has taught him how to be calm, although she doesn't always want to be close to him. They have like a typical grumpy aunt-boisterous nephew relationship!

My dogs have brought my family an immeasurable amount of joy but they have also been the cause of many quarrels — my wife still insists that Charcoal ate her white blouse whole — and the reason why we have less to spend on our vacations, amongst other things. Potential dog owners have to realise that you cannot have the cake without the calories; it comes together. Dogs can bring out the best and worst in us."

CELESTE AND TIMBER WITH OWNERS LIAM AND MYRA

> "I will not pass judgement on any owner who gives up their dog, as we may not be aware of their circumstances, but every person getting a dog should plan in advance as they will be with you for life. They are like your children. You wouldn't give up on your children regardless of circumstances, and neither should you with your dogs. You should have all contingencies worked out before you get one."

DR JADE KUA

#HomeIsWhere TheHeartIs

'OMG You're a dog person too!!!!' Jade and I exclaimed simultaneously, before breaking into doggie chatter, talking nineteen to a dozen about our beloved children.

In between the fashion show and the charity auction, we got talking about our respective furkids. "Did you adopt?" we both blurted out at the same time! Adoption is the new badge of honour indeed, and it was lovely to see the who's who of Singapore society coming together that night to support the animals.

Not only did Jade adopt her dogs, she has three! Her husband Emil and her have opened their hearts and their house to a trio of unfortunate canines. My heart broke when I heard their stories of how they loved unconditionally but were ultimately betrayed by all their previous owners.

"I got to hear of Bob Dylan and Bob Marley's plight through a mutual friend of their former owner. He was migrating from Singapore to New York and was unable to take the dogs with him. Our mutual friend was enlisted to help find new homes for the hounds.

BOB DYLAN BOB MARLEY CHUBBY

My then-fiancee and I were preparing for our wedding when we heard the news of their adoption, and decided to give these poor unfortunate dogs a loving forever home.

When I first met them, I was struck by how friendly they both were. My husband, Emil, is really good with dogs and helped them integrate really quickly into our household.

Although the two English Pointers are approximately the same age and look alike, they are not from the same litter. And they certainly have very different personalities!

Dylan loves his hugs and rub-downs and is the more affectionate one of the two. He has remained my good old faithful and loving companion through the years.

Marley, on the other hand, is the cheeky one. He'll snuggle with you until he realises you don't have any treats for him, then he'll saunter off in search of something else that's more interesting.

Despite their differences, both dogs are unconditional in their love and devotion to everyone in the family, and have even saved the life of one of us.

BOB DYLAN

I was pregnant with Mark one year after the dogs were adopted. The Bobs and I were relaxing in the basement one evening when they suddenly sprang up and started barking vociferously. They dashed out of the room towards the first level. I lumbered up, thinking they must have heard a stranger at the door. Instead, I found our very old Dalmatian in the pool. He had slipped in accidently and was whining ever so softly. I leapt into the pool immediately to help him out. We were all ever so grateful to the Bobs for saving his life.

The nine years since we adopted the dogs have just flown past. They have seen me through my three pregnancies and have taken to the kids really well. When I was pregnant, I would talk to both dogs and tell them how excited I was to have the babies. I asked them to help me look after the babies. Both dogs have become kind and understanding big brothers to the children, especially when the young ones accidently prod or hug them a little too exuberantly. They are not that patient with the adults, though, and do not take any nonsense

from us! They are also relatively fierce with strangers, making them great nannies as well as guard dogs! One day, whilst we were at the groomers, we heard of a husky in urgent need of a home. His owners had decided to split up and none of them wanted the dog. The groomer sent multiple desperate messages with the adoption notice, lest the innocent dog be put down. One of these messages reached me.

I was initially not interested. I was of the opinion that people who owned huskies in this tropical heat were thoughtless and insensitive, as they are cold climate dogs. However, it was through no fault of the dog that he ended up in Singapore. I was also really cross at the irresponsible ex-couple for giving up on their faithful friend. I have a very low opinion of such people indeed, especially if the poor dog is used as a bargaining pawn!

After a week with no response, and the possibility of the dog being euthanised became very real, I decided to take him home.

I did extensive research on the breed to make his stay with us as comfortable as possible. I made a promise that I will remain committed to him till the end. I felt a responsibility to atone for his previous owners' terrible treatment of him and vowed to make his life as happy as possible.

When I first brought him home, he was so sullen and disagreeable that I couldn't even put a leash around his neck to take him for a walk. Fortunately, my animal whisperer husband Emil was able to win him over and soon, they went for their first walk together rather peacefully.

It took him several weeks before he began to settle down. I was so worried that he wasn't eating enough, and feared that his experience with the ex-couple had scarred him for life. The Bobs tried to help as much as they could but Chubby generally kept to himself.

About five years ago, Chubby suffered a mild stroke that left him bedbound and frustrated. The vets had suggested amputation in case the legs grew sores, but my kids objected. Instead, they kept him company, sitting with him every single day, reading to him and entertaining him. My maids carried him out for fresh air and massaged his legs till one miraculous day, he got better. Today, his limp is barely noticeable and you can only see if when he runs.

Chubby has become a lot more affectionate since his attack. I think he is particularly grateful to everyone who cared for him, especially the kids and the maids.

When we got married, we didn't factor in the presence of three very different dogs sharing their lives with us.

When we first got the dogs, I was fearful that they would not adjust well. It is really traumatic for any dog to be given up, especially after having loved their owner

BOB MAYLEY

CHUBBY

unconditionally. In fact, the Bobs would look really lost whenever they see us going away with packed suitcases, and my heart breaks a little each time.

Our dogs are like our children. They have feelings, just like humans, and, like kids, they don't filter them. Their joy is amplified in their volley of barks and the smiles on their faces, and their sadness when we leave the house is written all over their faces.

We have welcomed the dogs into our home and they have trusted us with their lives. I could, and would never give up on them."

#You'reMy BestFriend

Joe is extremely passionate about rescue canines. It is a cause that is very close to his heart, and he has never hesitated to galvanise his fan base and use his connections to assist any dog in need.

When we rescued Kylie, the poodle with a broken leg, I needed to start a crowdfund campaign to raise money for her surgery and convalescence, Joe solved it with one Whats App message and two shakes of a ducks tail, and we managed to raise the amount in a week!

Joe has an adopted goldie, a young dog that had an unfairly rough start in life.

"I adopted Mojo when he was a mere year and a half. At that tender age, when dogs were supposed to be just getting into their own and developing their personality, Mojo spent his early years being passed from one owner to another. The poor dog never had a chance to experience a proper childhood..

His first owner hung on to him for a year. The family treated him like a play dog and gave him up when he grew too big for them. A second family then adopted Mojo, but because he did not receive proper coaching as a young puppy, he was hyper active and would behave like a little puppy, even though he was full grown. He would pounce on the family's children during play and the family did not know how to control him. Fearing for their children's safety, they decided to put Mojo up for adoption again.

I chanced upon his adoption post on Facebook and made an enquiry. I had just moved into my new place six months earlier,

MOJO

and felt that the time was right for me to have a furry friend to share the space with me. Sadly, I was too late and he had been passed to someone else already. In a strange twist of fate, his second owner contacted me a few weeks later to inform me that Mojo was up for adoption yet again! The new owner could not handle his madcap personality and gave up on him.

I remember meeting Mojo the first time at the home of the family. He was in pretty bad shape, very skinny with really patchy skin. But he was extremely hyper. In another life, he would have easily been an over-charged energizer bunny! I remember him pouncing on me and peeing on my feet when he met me. The owner apologised, but I knew at that very moment that I wanted Mojo. We connected instantly, and I found him very endearing,

On the 2 May 2015, 18-month old Mojo officially came into my life. I was his fourth owner.

Everyday happened like a whirlwind. He celebrated his new life with a spectacular pee and poo the minute he ran into my home. Absolutely memorable indeed!

"
Be responsible to take care of not only the basic well-being of the dog, but also be present as a parent, to look after their health and discipline. Having a dog is a lifelong commitment, if you are not sure, don't commit to having one. Because a dog sees you as their one and only life commitment, and when you don't, it breaks their heart.
"

JOE TAN

He had a lot of firsts with me. I changed his diet and started feeding him proper dog food. I brought him for a thorough grooming session and started on a regiment to help him clear his skin. He shed a lot at his first grooming session, which spoke volumes about how he was cared for in his previous homes. He fell ill and I had to help him clear his tick infestation

Toilet training was easy. He was used to being outdoors so it was relatively painless to handle his potty needs without leaving (too much of) a mess at home.

I taught him how to walk on a leash calmly beside me. That took me the better part of four months to achieve. But he's extremely smart and can pick up immediately if you are an inexperienced dog walker. If you're new to the leash, be prepared to fly!

He showed signs of separation anxiety so I had to teach him how to be independent and not panic when I was not around. But when I'm home, he is the most spoilt dog in the whole world, always yearning for attention.

I remember there were days when I would get upset over work, and he would sense it immediately. He would lean against my leg and rest his head on my thigh, as if to tell me that he's there for me, and that immediately made me feel better.

Many people, when they meet the new, improved, handsome Mojo with his soft, silky, golden coat trailing behind him, are shocked to find out he was adopted Not all purchased dogs are perfect and neither are adopted dogs imperfect. Most, if not all, dog problems stem from human negligence, cruelty or ignorance. I have never had the inclination to purchase any of my dogs. I had my first dog, the sweetest Miniature Retriever named Sally, when I was 10. I was taught to handle her at that tender young age, and she was very well behaved. She was adopted, and I have always believed ever since in taking that route with all my dogs.

I do have a list of criteria whenever I look for a dog to adopt. It is important that I find one that suits my lifestyle and can adapt to my schedule and demands of my work. You must also be knowledgeable about the breed, in order to give them the most appropriate nutrition and meet their basic health and exercise needs.

At the end of the day, purchased or adopted, it takes a lot of hard work and patience for a dog to turn out this way. Pet shop purchases are not a surefire guarantee that the dogs are healthy, but regardless, every dog will thrive on love and the proper care.

Mojo is testament to that.

I spend a lot of time and effort on him. I make sure I give him the right food, enough clean drinking water, proper grooming, I protect him from getting ticks or other diseases and bring him on walks each day to exercise him and tire him out. That has, honestly, been my biggest challenge. Mojo is a ball of energy, and sometimes, because of my walk, I tire myself out inadvertently instead!

Mojo is my boy, my son. I loved him the moment I met him. He has been a handful for me, but I find my relationship with him extremely fulfilling. I do feel guilty on many occasions, when work occupies my days and I am unable to spend as much time as I want with him. But I absolutely appreciate how loyal he is. I remember all those nights when I had to work overtime at home. He would sit beside me patiently, waiting for me to finish before I walk him. It is because of Mojo that I have stopped hanging out late, preferring to come back home, and also to ensure that I cater time to walk him every day.

When I got married in January 2019, Mojo took pride of place as my wing man, leading the procession and helping to officiate the ceremony.

Looking at this handsome boy, and watching him look back at me, I know that every single obstacle we crossed only drew us closer. If you ask me if it was worth it, it is most definitely an emphatic yes."

❝

**Growing up with pets has taught me responsibility,
empathy and unconditional love.**

❞

VERONICA ZHANG

#ThePursuit OfHappiness

Leia and The Phat Dogs, a trio of hip Huskies, met when they were all models in a doggie runway show. The first time we saw the dogs was a most surreal experience. At seven in the morning, backlit by the soft rays of the morning sun, their soft fur rippling gently in slow-mo as they walked, the three dogs looked like a soft-focused scene from a Spaghetti Western.

The pack was almost upon us when we noticed little Bailey, a diminutive Springer Spaniel, trailing behind. "That's the model" said his proud pawrent. The rest of the dogs are just here to cheer him on.

As luck would have it, a couple of dogs were pulled from the show due to circumstances beyond everyone's control, leaving a vacancy for three additional models. The Huskies turned out to be naturals and rocked the show, almost like they were born for the catwalk.

All four of Veronica's dogs are rescues. She adopted all of them at fairly advanced stages in their lives.

It is an old myth that the dog/owner bonding starts from puppyhood. It is also untrue that senior dogs are more stubborn or harder to train compared to puppies. Dogs are highly adaptable. While it is true that some adopted dogs come with personal baggage or health issues, it can be the same with store bought puppies. In both cases, time is required to understand and train them.

Unknown to many, mature or senior dogs are actually more suitable for the working class because of their low activity level. They also do not require as much attention as puppies and they do not ruin your furniture! When adopting, look beyond the appearance; the personality of the pet is what matters. Appearance can be improved over time with some tender loving care.

"We have a preference to rescue huskies because they are a very misunderstood breed. Many people buy them because they are so adorable as puppies, but they grew to become angry teenagers when they have insufficient exercise or if the owner is not firm. Huskies are one of the most difficult breeds to rehome because of their size, character and the high maintenance required to care for their coat."

LOKI
COCO
OZZY
BAILEY

Loki, the eldest, was her first rescue. He was a senior, adopted from the SPCA, who lived in Veronica's neighbourhood. Unfortunately for him, he had an owner who did not care much for him. He was always kept in the front yard, and would watch the family's shenenigans sadly from outside the house.

"We always felt it was quite inhumane to keep a husky outdoor without a fan. At times the front yard will be unkempt for days with pee and poo around. It was well known in the neighbourhood that Loki was a neglected husky; neighbours would feed and pet him."

By a stroke of fate, the owner had to move back to New Zealand for work. Needless to say, Loki did not feature in his relocation plans. Soon, word got around the neighbourhood that Loki was up for adoption.

"I think Loki played a big role in rescuing himself. Huskies are generally quite aloof, but Loki was friendly and receptive and tried very hard to impress us. I used to take Genki, my late husky to visit Loki whenever we walked around the neighbourhood. They would sniff each other and wag their tails. My family always felt bad for Loki whenever we saw him because he seemed so lonely.

We just couldn't leave him knowing he will be sent back to the SPCA if he was not adopted.

I arranged a meeting with the owner to learn more about his dog. I wanted to understand more about Loki's age and health before taking him.

There were several things that set off my alarm bells immediately. Firstly, Loki was very badly groomed; there were no vaccination and medical record and thirdly, he was coughing rather badly.

I insisted the owners take him for a medical check before deciding if we want to adopt him. It turned out Loki was severely underweight and heartworm positive."

Veronica's vet was very concerned about her adoption plans. Loki was estimated to be about eight, and the prognosis was poor. Genki had just passed and she was concerned that they would be subjected to another heartbreak. However, Veronica was very reluctant to leave him in the unloving home and negligent owner.

The family discussed his adoption.

"My parents visited Loki every single evening and interacted with him through the gate. Loki responded and bonded very well with my Dad and he would look forward to seeing him. My parents recorded their interaction with Loki and I was utterly gutted that he was so neglected. After a week, I decided that even if we could not spend years with Loki, he deserved a loving and a warm home to spend his last days. I texted the owner to arrange a meeting to pick the dog up. However, he was too busy and couldn't be bothered, so he told me to pick him up myself. He did not even show up to say goodbye. Once I told the owner we had collected Loki, he became unresponsive to all future messages."

Loki was ecstatic when he finally left his hellhole of a previous home; he walked with a skip in his step and wagged his tail non-stop. Loki walked through the gate of his new house with ease, but was hesitant to enter the house. Veronica had to coax and guide him using the leash. He also refused to enter the kitchen or the backyard, which (everyone suspected) could have stemmed from an unpleasant memory.

(L-R)
LOKI, COCO, OZZY

He was also successfully treated for heartworm, although the recovery period of two months proved to be rather challenging. Being grass trained, he needed to conduct his business outdoors, so Veronica would put Loki on a trolley and push him around the neighbourhood. He hopped on and off whenever he needed.

"Loki's sweet nature helped us ease the pain of losing Genki, it was almost like he knew we were mourning. We found it amazing that Loki's favourite spot in the house was also Genki's. He also knew instinctively that the food on the coffee table was off-limits, something we trained Genki to recognise"

Sometime in October 2015, whilst on business in Australia, Veronica stumbled across an adoption notice on Facebook for two huskies, a mother and son duo. The post resurfaced on Christmas Eve, when she had returned to Singapore. She contacted the re-homer and arranged a viewing.

Loki was relaxed and slept well on the first night.

The family spent the first month interacting with him. Bit by bit, they got to know his habits and idiosyncrasies. They received no help from his previous owner, who seemed to have washed his hands off this dog. Veronica tried to groom Loki and brush out his mattered and unruly fur but he would squirm and run away. He did not like being touched and hugged. It was also tough to put a leash on him. Loki would tremble if anyone touched his hind legs or his stomach. Through patience and lots of love, they gradually earned his trust. Soon, even the neighbours began to notice the very visible improvement in Loki.

"Loki fitted into our family quite easily. He enjoys spending time outside, people-watching and sun bathing. We would leave him on the verandah with a big fan and he would join us inside the house when he was done with the outdoors."

Coco was a retired show-dog who was also used for breeding, and Ozzy was her son. The previous owners adopted them directly from the breeders. Both dogs were de-barked by the breeder because they were kept in a tiny space with lots of other huskies. The previous owners had to rehome them because they couldn't care for Coco and Ozzy any longer. Both dogs were not to be separated, which proved to be rather difficult for the owners. Most people were only interested in taking Coco, but not Ozzy.

Before Veronica got to the rehomer, both dogs were adopted by a guy who promised to care for them and keep them indoors. However, it was discovered that the dogs were left outdoors in an unkempt environment, so they were taken back. That was when Veronica knew the dogs were meant to be hers.

"It was love at first sight when I saw them! Coco was very sweet and friendly, but Ozzy was wary of strangers. I wanted to take them home immediately, but was uncertain if we could manage three Huskies in the household. However, the possibility that they might end up in different families was heartbreaking so we decided on a home trial.

We took Loki to meet Coco and Ozzy. I was so relieved that he was very receptive. When we went to the car, Coco dashed into the backseat and refused to come out.

We always felt that she chose to adopt us."

Coco and Ozzy went home with Veronica for a home trial that very day! The owners handed over their towels, feeding bowls and food to help ease the transition. The owners requested for frequent photo updates of Coco and Ozzy whilst the rehomer requested for Ozzy to be sterilized.

"It was like Coco and Ozzy already knew we were going to be their new owners; they were very well behaved and calm on the journey home. Coco roamed the house happily, but Ozzy was nervous and tagged behind very closely. They began drinking lots of water after they discovered the free-flowing pet water fountain. Loki sat at his usual spot and observed them."

Veronica did not get any sleep on the first night because Coco and Ozzy were extremely nervous and did not sleep. After they calmed down and got used to the environment, Ozzy suddenly began to hump Coco!

"I spent the whole night trying to prevent that. We took them on a few long walks the next day to wear them out and they were able to have a few short naps during the day, but whenever I laid their towels down, Ozzy had the urge to hump Coco again! On the third night, I had a hunch that he might have been trained to do so, so I removed the towels. They two dogs slept soundly next to each other with no hanky panky!"

Veronica and her family spent Christmas Eve bathing the dogs, trimming their nails, cleaning their ears and brushing their mattered coats through the night. Her priority was to unclog their skin from the dry shampoo residue that was stuck on their skin.

"It took a lot of brushing and a few baths to clear up the skin. Ozzy's skin condition was worse than expected; there were spots oozing with pus and he would attract houseflies when we brushed him outdoors. The easy way out would have been to shave him down, but I didn't want to damage his coat further. I simply trimmed the fur in the problematic areas to make cleaning and the application of medication easier. It took at least an hour every night over the course of a year for him to fully recover. Ozzy also had prostate inflammation and was peeing blood. The day he had surgery to be neutered was the first time Coco was ever separated from him. She was restless the entire day and waited at the door for his return."

During the initial days, Ozzy drank so much water that he could not eat his dinner. "I assumed it was because water intake was restricted in the previous household. I had to take them on 12 pee breaks per day because they drank so much."

Veronica stayed home during the first month to supervise the interaction and play between the three dogs. The first time she left the house for a doctor visit, Ozzy whined and cried even though her Mom stayed home with him. "I realised that he might have separation anxiety and tried to rectify it gradually."

The two weeks flew by and Veronica decided to adopt the dogs. They were registered with AVA, and Veronica started the long process of addressing their health issues as well as toilet and leash training.

However, in week three, something happened that threatened to derail all of Veronica's hard work. Coco and Loki got into a fight. Loki suffered puncture wounds on this snout and front paw, while Coco got a smaller puncture wound on her front paw. Veronica's sister's finger required nine stitches. A week later, it was Ozzy's turn to fight with Loki. Both of Loki's ears were torn at the edges and his ears remains kinked today.

"The fights were captured by our home surveillance camera so we could identify the triggers. I was pressured by my family to give up Coco and Ozzy after the altercations. I tried very hard to convince my family that I would be able to work with them to prevent future incidents. I studied pack behaviour, learnt about the triggers that lead to dogfights and how to identify calming signals. It is never the dogs' fault but the humans who have put them in that situation. I identified the causes for the fights. It stemmed from jealousy and hierarchy of attention within the pack. Coco wanted to assert dominance to be pack leader whilst Ozzy was upset that I gave Loki extra attention. I took three months away from work and spent all day supervising and enforcing boundaries within the pack. I observed that Loki was undeterred after the fights, so I helped him rise to the pack leader

position with encouragement. Coco was put into second place; she was taught to respect Loki. It wasn't easy for her because she has always been Ozzy's leader their whole lives.

We had to let Loki be first in everything even if he didn't want to, from feeding to brushing, walking and drinking, so that Coco and Ozzy could identify that Loki is given priority. I had to distance myself from Ozzy and let my folks handle him so he knows that I do not "belong" to him exclusively. It was very stressful training them and extremely emotional dealing with my family. It is not very often that my decisions are not supported and I had to stand up to them. I could tell that it was a very stressful and tiring period for Coco and Ozzy as well. I am very glad that we persevered to stay together. Eventually, Coco and Ozzy also managed to regain my family's trust that they are not aggressive dogs."

Biting does not always equate with aggression; it is also a form of expression for dogs. Coco and Ozzy probably had to resort to biting because they were debarked and it was the only way they could express displeasure.

With time, the pack managed to learn mutual trust. Coco and Ozzy respected Loki's boundaries and hence developed a strong pack mentality.

"We never had another fight."

Loki, Coco and Ozzy have an unbreakable bond now. Loki has since risen to the role of pack leader. He may be the smallest in size amongst the three but he is the protector of the pack. If other dogs barked at Coco and Ozzy, he would immediate protect them by barking back, especially when he realised that they are not capable of barking back.

Loki would also help train all subsequent fosters. He corrects habits that Veronica frowns upon and would bark whenever the dogs are breaking house rules. Loki used to be quite vocal, but he toned down after he realised that Coco and Ozzy are debarked. When Loki barks or howls today, we know that it is urgent and requires immediate attention.

BAILEY

"Ozzy and I bonded over the nights I spent cleaning up his skin. I helped him gain confidence to become the sociable dog today; he readily accepts pets and he would give kisses."

Ozzy has not had any skin issues since his recovery and now has the lushest coat amongst the pack.

"I never expected that rehabilitating and nursing dogs will be such a rewarding experience. To see them healthy, being loved and socialising with other dogs and humans warms my heart. All the effort that we put into training and caring for them is reflected in our dogs' behaviour and appearance."

Oh, and what of Bailey, the original model?

Before he embarked on his catwalk career, Bailey (formerly named Blake) was a Narcotic Detector Dog from the Singapore Police Force. Veronica found out about his retirement on Facebook and decided they were ready for another dog.

"We felt that our pack is not balanced. Coco and Ozzy were always together in their own world, whether playing or sleeping. Loki was a loner because he couldn't get involved in their activities. In fact, no other dogs could get involved in during their playtime. Coco and Ozzy would sniff the butts of the other dogs, but would not initiate or respond to play."

The Para-Vet recommended Bailey and it was love at first sight. He was a jovial little fella who fitted perfectly with the pack and recognised Loki as the pack's alpha. He began following Loki from the word go.

"We were very impressed with his pack behaviour and couldn't wait for him to come home with us."

Bailey was very disciplined from the very first day. The family only

Coco used to only fend for Ozzy, but after bonding with Loki, she has became the pack's mother. Due to her sweet nature, Coco is very popular with the children in the neighbourhood. Coco is also extremely clean and rather OCD. She has never had any potty accidents in the house. "She would try her best to wake me up (in the middle of the night) to take her outside. It's like she takes pride in keeping the house clean. Coco used to be so proud that she does not eat scraps of her treats if they fell out of her mouth onto the floor!

"She consoles and offers her kisses when I'm feeling sad."

Ozzy is the pack's food connoisseur. He chooses the treats for the pack, especially for Loki, the fussiest eater of the three. Despite being debarked, Ozzy is ever alert and has learnt to use what's left of his voice to guard the house.

needed to enforce toilet and leash training. He started off as a one-man's dog, but quickly began to bond with the other family members by the third month. When the pack bonded with the other family members by the third month, Bailey was almost the pack's protector; when the pack was off-leash at the dog park, Bailey will shoo away the birds or cats because he knew the Huskies would give chase and ultimately get reprimanded.

BAILEY WITH SPECIAL NEEDS ARTIST, SIJUN, AND BFF, LEIA

"We did not teach him this behaviour and were astounded by it."

Due to Bailey's previous training in the K9 unit, he loved to play with balls. With his help, Veronica taught Coco and Ozzy to play "fetch". It made their time in the park so much more enjoyable.

"We were flabbergasted that he was able to fall into the role of a submissive within the pack so perfectly. In public, he never cared that the Huskies had more attention than him; in fact he has never warmed up to strangers. Bailey was contented being our little lap dog at home. He bonded especially with Loki. If Loki was napping in the front porch, Bailey would bark to let him know that dinner is ready. When it was bedtime, Bailey would run up the stairs, but quickly come back down to accompany Loki up. Loki had age-related arthritis and could not move as fast as the other dogs."

With the introduction of Bailey, the pack opened up and began playing with other dogs in the dog park.

Alls well, unfortunately, did not end well with this pack. It took an unfortunate, tragic turn on the morning of 9 May 2018.

I remember getting an urgent text message from my doggie group that morning. "Bailey is lost! Here are the details. Please help repost."

73

We kept getting more information and updates throughout the day. The entire group was mobilised to search for him. Each group reached out to their own respective circle too, and several search parties were organised. Those at work began to make plans to take the evening shift. We were frantic with worry and anxiety.

As time passed, a feeling of foreboding began to envelope several of us.

"On that fateful morning, at about 3am, my dad took the dogs out for their usual morning pee break. Ozzy was doing his business, and Bailey seemed impatient, so my dad relaxed his grip on his leash. It was his usual pee spot, barely 200m from the house, but it was a secluded and poorly lit area.

The dogs would usually complete their pee and take a walk to the nearby playground. However, Bailey did not return that morning. Dad woke us all up and we began combing the area. I searched the playground and our usual spots in the neighbourhood. My Dad searched the entire secluded spot where Bailey was last sighted. But he was nowhere to be found.

By mid-morning, we had covered well over 20km by foot. I had a stick to comb through the thick vegetation, in case Bailey was trapped. Gavin, a fellow dog lover, saw my post on facebook and offered to help. He brought along his retired K9 and trekked the path that Bailey was last sighted and went as far as the CTE. His Belgian Shepard was unable to pick up Bailey's scent beyond his usual pee spot.

We were puzzled. For Bailey to run off, he would first have to pass by the house. All the dogs are trained to recognise the way home via different walking routes. Bailey could even identify our car at any car park.

I speculated that a vehicle might have picked Bailey up because he loved car rides. I filed reports with AVA, SPCA, NEA, EMAS and LTA, in the hope that I would be notified if Bailey had gotten into an accident.

Close to noon, I received news that he was sighted as road kill at the CTE near the Seletar exit. I did not want to believe it and hoped against hope that it was a hoax.

Eventually, I received the dreaded call from AVA. They picked up Bailey's carcass at around 2.30pm. I made a trip down to AVA. I went numb when I opened the black bag to see Bailey's cold and limp body inside. I recognised his bow-legged front legs. I picked up his collar, stained with blood and I knew I could no longer lie to myself. The staff at AVA were very helpful and understanding; without their assistance and advice, I would be at a loss. They advised me to send Bailey to a crematorium instead of taking him home, due to biohazard issues. It was the worst day of my life.

After the accident, we did a futile search for holes along the fence that skirted the expressway. We took different routes because we wanted to understand how he got onto CTE. We are still baffled and, until today, do not have the answer.

Bailey's demise changed the pack dynamics greatly. Losing a pack member has made them more united and their bond with us has also grown stronger. Coco and Ozzy wanted to join me on the search for Bailey that morning. However, they did not last long under the heat. Whenever I came home to fill my water bottle, I would find Coco and Ozzy waiting by the gate for Bailey's return. Loki stayed in his little corner, depressed. When I left for AVA to identify Bailey's body, it was almost as if Ozzy knew that Bailey has passed away. He started howling and crying. Coco joined in, and Loki started tearing.

When we took our walk on the night of the accident, for some unknown reason, the pack wanted to walk towards the CTE. Ozzy was marking more along the way, which was unusual because he rarely marks. It was as if he wanted to leave a scent trail home for Bailey.

The three dogs became each other's support system. Ozzy took up the role of Loki's cuddle buddy, whilst Coco became Loki's wingman; waiting for him at the stairs at bedtime and sunbathing with him. Loki used to sleep in my parent's bedroom with Bailey, but he has refused to enter the bedroom since then. Loki sleeps in my bedroom now, in-between Coco and Ozzy. Perhaps they could sense his loneliness.

All three huskies were very depressed. Despite visits from human and doggie friends, they remained restless and uninterested. In the first month following Bailey's demise, the pack lost interest in eating and we had to cook different food to stimulate their appetite. At the dog park, they were uninterested in playing with their doggy friends. Initially I attributed it to the weather, but I later realised that they might still be missing their goofy pack mate. Coco has refused to play 'fetch' till today; it almost seems like she has totally lost interest in playing with balls. When they are off-leash in the dog park, the pack would pay very close attention to us and maintain constant eye contact.

Currently, the Huskies are not allowed to walk around the area that Bailey was last sighted. We make sure we always have absolute control over them, no matter how safe or brightly lit the conditions may be. We keep an extra tight

hold on the leashes when we pick up their poop to prevent losing sight on them and keep a vigilant watch to ensure there are no cats in the vicinity.

My dad feels the greatest guilt of losing Bailey. He bore the brunt of the blame from my Mom and myself. I was in an emotional turmoil because my Dad loved the dogs as much as myself; so to blame him would be unfair. My parents chose to walk the dogs because they loved to bond with the pack during the walks. After a discussion with my Mom, we chose to support my Dad and soldier through this period of distress together as a family.

I have also asked him not to slow down his car or pick us up when he sees us during our walks. I am training the pack to pay less attention and be less *excited when cars stop in front of them. Hopefully this will help them should there be a situation when a stranger's car stops to pick them up.*

We had red and swollen eyes every day from crying. We would get emotional whenever we take our walks with the pack around the neighbourhood. It was a tremendously difficult period of our lives. It took us eight months before we can put away Bailey's bed and belongings. My family and I are taking time to mourn at our own pace; we did not hold any celebrations at home for a year because we just couldn't.

I have told myself to make everyday count with these kiddos because they are already seniors and we are disadvantaged on time. They will always get the walkies and cuddles no matter how busy I am. I have no regrets on the time and quality of life spent with Bailey, but it was how he died that pained me greatly and this will

> **"**
>
> **It is crucial to license your pet; the microchip is useless if licenses are not renewed because the authorities would be unable to link the lost pet to you. We would love to think of our dogs as our highly intelligent, obedient, disciplined fur kids; but at the end of the day, they are also just instinctive animals. In spite of the training and discipline instilled in them, they still require close monitoring outdoors.**
>
> **"**
>
> VERONICA ZHANG

forever change how my family deals with our dogs. Losing Bailey made me cherish the pack even more; they used to only get car rides on weekends, but now they get car rides whenever I'm free! There can never be enough time with them.

I would never in my wildest nightmare expect that we would lose a precious family member due to negligence; Bailey's excellent behaviour was totally taken for granted."

On 31 January 2019, Ozzy was diagnosed with Megaesophagus and Myasthenia Gravis.

During his weakest days, Ozzy was unable to walk from the door to the front yard and was incontinent. He was too weak to take the stairs, so we camped out in the living room, with him, sleeping right beside him so we could assist him when he regurgitated.

The pack's lifestyle and diet was changed to accommodate Ozzy. We started feeding them small meals with tender meats, fruit juice or bone broth gelatine blocks and took short, but more frequent walks. Ozzy and I would sit at the park while Loki and Coco walked. That way, Ozzy could still participate in his pack activities, which he loved doing. We tried to include Ozzy in everything we do so that he didn't miss out.

Loki was by Ozzy's side all the time, supporting him. His mother Coco was stressed and hid in a corner, monitoring her son's condition from a distance.

During the worst of it, Ozzy was taking six different medications a day. He received six painful injections during one of his vet visits. He was a brave trooper who did not once whine, even though he was suffering.

On 22 May, he rapidly declined. We rushed him into emergency. I received a phone call at 6.40am on 23 May that Ozzy has passed away.

We decided to bring Loki and Coco to send Ozzy off, hoping that this would give them closure so they don't keep searching and waiting for him to come home. Loki and Coco have grown closer since Ozzy's demise.

We felt a great sense of loss from Ozzy's departure. Losing two fur babies consecutively has put a major strain on everyone's hearts.

We hope that he is in a better place now, free from pain and with Bailey as company.

"

A dog is the only thing on earth that loves you more than he loves himself.

"

JOSH BILLINGS

> ❝
> *If a man aspires towards a*
> *righteous life, his first act of abstinence*
> *is from injury to animals.*
> ❞

ALBERT EINSTEIN

#ChainReaction

On 4 July 2018, I chanced upon a post on the VFA Facebook page that spoke of a dog they had just bailed out from AVA. He had been surrendered to the authorities by his previous owner for being aggressive. What made this case different from all the other disgusting abandonment stories centered around a padlock attached to a too-tight choke chain around his neck. According to the post, the owner used it to secure the chain around his neck as it was too loose (I reckoned it probably belonged to another – bigger – dog and they were too frugal to buy a new chain that was size appropriate for their smaller dog). The key to the padlock was misplaced so they couldn't remove it when he was surrendered. The good folks from VFA had to use a cutter to cut it open, but it left a dark ring around his neck, a visual reminder of that horrific act.

I couldn't get my mind off the dishevelled tangled bedraggled mess that was the terrier. He hung his head low and looked downcast and crestfallen and I was glad he was now in the safe hands of the shelter folks.

Fast forward to a VFA adoption drive in Pasir Ris at the end of the month. I had popped down to lend a hand, and was acquainting myself with the animals when I noticed a solitary dog separated from the rest of the pack. "He's aggressive", some of the volunteers remarked. I recognised him from the dark ring around his neck, but left him alone.

Day 2 of the drive and I found him wandering round the shaded enclosure which housed the bichons, poodles and schnauzers. He sauntered up to me, stuck his head into my crotch and rested his head against my thigh. "Novel way to get to know someone" I thought. "Be careful, he will bite", the volunteers advised ominously, but being attacked was the last thing on my mind. I found it hard to associate the word aggressive with this lovable little pooch. Still, I proceeded with caution.

I found out that the shelter had re-named him Kenzo. It was a tradition for them to change the names of all their rescues. It was almost ritualistic, to help them erase the traumatic memories of their past and symbolically give them a fresh start in life.

Kenzo and I met several more times over the course of the next few months. He would come tottering over each time I visited the shelter, and we quickly bonded. He was SOLO the sweetest, gentlest creature with the most adorable eyes and a cheeky grin, and he would always welcome me by giving me his paw. But I also witnessed his so-called 'aggression in action, directed both at other dogs and the shelter volunteers. But it wasn't aggression. It was a defence mechanism, borne from the traumatic abuse in his previous household. He was terrified of umbrellas and there were trigger points near his butt, so we suspected he was beaten there with a brolly. He was also extremely aggrieved by a certain demographic of people, so we could guess the profile of his previous owner.

"

There are no perfect dogs but with love and patience, they can learn how to live in our world. Shelter dogs have almost always had very difficult former lives, but give them a second chance. All they need is time. Dog bites are just superficial wounds. They will heal. So will the dog's broken spirit, eventually. Don't be afraid of them. Dogs are only aggressive cos man made them so. Keep trying until you gain their trust...
Whether you adopt a shelter dog or purchased yours, please take good care of them. Be a responsible dog owner. Always make time for your dog, no matter what. They will never give up on you so please do not give up on them.

"

DENISE AND DANIEL

I knew not to blame him, and tried to make him as comfortable and loved as I could. I prayed hard for the right family to adopt him, someone who was patient, loving and willing to invest time and effort into helping him.

Denise and Daniel had read about an adoption drive from a Facebook post, and showed up that faithful weekend in October. I was shadowing a senior volunteer, learning the ropes of screening potential adopters when our paths crossed. They were not sure if they were ready to adopt, as Daniel's dog, a Chihuahua who had been with him for 14 years, had recently crossed the rainbow bridge, but they were drawn to Kenzo. Being responsible dog owners, they decided to sleep on it to make sure they were absolutely ready to commit. They took a break, went on an anniversary holiday and contacted the shelter when they returned.

I remember getting that text message one fateful Sunday asking if I would like to be there for the handover. It gave me a chance to say goodbye to him. Kenzo seemed to know he was leaving the shelter. He cradled his head in my lap and gave me a reassuring lick, as if to say 'I'm going to be ok. I'm a big boy and I can take care of myself'. He was calm and cooperative, and even celebrated his adoption with a farewell poop at the entrance to the shelter before being driven off to his new home.

"When he first set foot in our home, we slowly walked him around the house, then unleashed him to let him get used to the surroundings. We gave him food and drink and tried not to stress him too much. We gave him free rein to roam around the house.

Thankfully he was toilet trained.

The first day was smooth; we spent most of it trying to get to know each other.

We bathed him on the second day; he

was as still as a block of wood. But he was beginning to trust us more and more. Daniel would bring him down frequently for walks to get used to his new surroundings and to bond with him."

I was so afraid it wasn't going to work out. Each time my phone beeped, I nervously hoped it wasn't bad news. But the first few messages were all hunky dory.

"This dog knows how to pee on paper, shake hands and sit when asked!"

"He functions really well on leash"

"He loves walking"

And then, one day, the dreaded text message appeared.

"We were both bitten by Kenzo."

My heart sank, but was reassured by the follow-up message.

"He needs more time to get used to us. Am trying to let him get used to his routine. But we didn't beat him. Don't worry. He is in good hands. All we want is for him to feel safe with us"

Any lesser human might not have reacted in such a calm, rational manner, and I gave a silent prayer of thanks for sending this beautiful couple Kenzo's way.

I popped in frequently to visit him and found a relaxed dog that was comfortable in his new surroundings. His true character started to emerge in time.

"We love that he is playful and hyperactive. We always end up playing catching with him. He can also be extremely manja but he is also very independent. We can leave him at home for hours on end and the house is still in one piece when we return!

He runs like a horse and jumps like a bunny. He loves to leap onto the dining table and lie flat like a sheepskin rug, observing us from his lofty perch. He is, however, terrified of thunder and the rain and would hide in our cabinets whenever it stormed.

He is also very greedy. He always seems to be hungry all of the time, and resource guards his food aggressively. We sometimes wonder if he was given enough to eat in his previous home.

We notice he loves car rides. He is always trying to peer through the windows and look at the surroundings. We took him on a drive down Orchard Road to look at the Christmas lights and the look of sheer joy and excitement on his face was so rewarding.

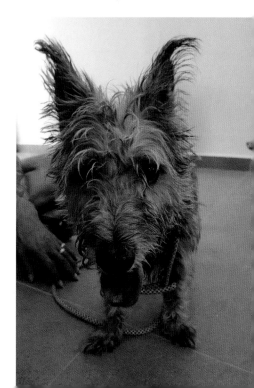

"Cleaning his ears is a real challenge, though. Denise and Daniel were not successful and were at the receiving end of his painful snapping each time they tried. Still, they tried to take things slow with positive association by rewarding him each time.

They also renamed him Solo. Quite an apt name for a dog that worked best as the only canine in the household.

When they felt that Solo had assimilated himself comfortably into the household, they brought him to see a vet. It turned out to be an extremely traumatic experience for the dog. He had to be sedated twice after continuing to struggle like a wild animal after the first. Three vet techs assisted in holding him down. He was defensive, traumatised and retaliated aggressively. My heart sank when I heard this, and beat myself up for not insisting hard enough that they consult my regular vet instead. Not every doctor can handle rescues. With Solo, restraining him only brought back painful memories and I'm sure all the horrific experiences came flooding back to him that very day.

It was back to square one after that day. He was back to his old self. It was very disappointing for the couple, especially after they had patiently invested so much time and effort, showering him with love and trying to make the relationship work. But they didn't give up and vowed to increase their efforts and triple the love to regain his trust.

"Cleaning his ears after the vet visit was impossible. He snapped whenever we try to get near. He was totally uncooperative and we couldn't do anything.

I was really afraid of getting bitten whilst cleaning his ear but we were left with only two choices – either bring him back to a vet who couldn't handle him to be cleaned every day, with the definite possibility of traumatizing him even further, or cleaning his ears ourselves.

I thought of wrapping my hands with a thick towel while holding on to a treat so his attention will be diverted, and clean his ear with the other. Our reaction would have to be fast as he is lightning quick and continued to snap. We had to stay calm and create a positive experience for him, making him realise that ear cleaning sessions would result in many treats."

After a long while, with lots of patience and tender loving care, they finally succeeded, and reported proudly one day that they can now clean his ears without having to bribe him with treats. What a great accomplishment for the wonderful pawrents.

I woke up one morning to the following text. *"Hey Daniel. Morning! He has been the sweetest thing so far, you have to meet him soon to see the difference in temperament."* And I knew that, for this one dog, his life has completely changed for the better.

#K9LoveAffair

Dilys and her family welcomed the beautiful Puska into their home in 2017.

Puska started life as a retired service dog who served in the Singapore Police Force K9 unit as a sniffer dog. Both narcotic and explosive detection dogs are trained to sniff for narcotics and explosive chemicals respectively. Spaniels and labradors are usually selected as sniffer dogs and they are chosen based on their traits and ability to work. Most of them are imported from special kennels overseas. Puska started life in the United Kingdom and travelled to Singapore as a young pup. When it was time for her to retire at the age of seven, she was put up for adoption, and her path crossed with that of the family Nair.

"When we finally decided our family circumstances were right to welcome a dog to the family, we considered buying a puppy from a breeder. After speaking with dog families and through our online research, we quickly turned to the idea of adoption. We had heard one too many horror stories about unethical breeders and decided not to go down that route. Having friends who adopted retired police working dogs helped us understand the process of adopting, and we made the necessary inquiries.

We first came to know about Puska when the K-9 unit informed us of three dogs due for retirement and provided us with their 'bios'.

The sense of excitement in the car was really quite palpable as we made the trip to the K9 unit to meet with the three dogs one sunny day in June. The realisation that the day would change our family made it quite a special outing indeed.

We met the dogs – two male chocolate labs and a black female lab. It was not easy deciding on who we would bring home. I wanted to bring all three back with me! I was most concerned for the fate of the other two dogs if we only chose one. What was to become of them if they were not adopted? The unit assured us that they would be loved and well taken care of till someone brought them home.

Puska was the most measured of the three dogs. She was thoughtful and gentle compared to the other two, who were excited and couldn't wait to be brought out to the field for a game of catch. We were taken in by her gentle nature and knew she was the one we would welcome to our family.

PUSKA

The first day must have been hard for Puska, the shy girl that she is. We were mindful to arrange her homecoming at a time when we could be at home for the entire day. She hid in the bushes in the garden for the first two days! She found her safe place in-between the vegetation where she could hide from us. It must have been quite a terrifying experience for her, having been in the K9 unit most of her life. But a ball did the trick, and, before long, she ventured out, maybe lured by the game of catch. I think that helped break the ice. Her old crate served as her bed for the first few weeks. Perhaps the familiarity of it helped ease any anxieties.

Being at home the first few days also helped with the toilet training and she quickly got used to the garden. There were a few accidents, though, which was to be expected. She probably mistook the carpet for the grass and discharged on it. We have since changed the carpet!

We made sure that we established a routine for her. We decided who would do the morning and evening walks and feeds, and her baths as well. She quickly fell into a good regiment for her pees and poos and there were no further accidents. Her training as a police dog meant that we had no problems with leash training and would walk by our side when we took her out. She loves to play with balls and you'll find a number around the house at any one point.

A number of people who heard we've adopted a retired police dog have asked if there's a difference between this and adopting a street dog or an ex-breeding dog. I think all dogs are the same, and will become attached to the family if treated with the right amount of love and commitment. As the K9 dogs tend to be larger breeds, they require their space to exercise and play. One must be prepared to invest time and effort to make sure they get their daily dose.

People think she's fierce and assume she'd make a good guard dog. On the contrary, she is nothing like that. She's shy when around both people and dogs, but wonderfully close and committed to our family. She's so scared of thunder and lightning, she would jump on the sofa, chair or bed and hide her head behind our backs. She loves to be scratched behind her ears and tummy and would paw at the hand when you stop, egging you on to continue. She loves a game of catch and often takes a ball in her mouth when she goes on her daily walks. Ex-K9s should be treated as a member of the family and never as a guard dog!

Life has changed so much since she came into our lives, in a similar way life changed when Sarah came along. With Puska, we have to work around her walks and meals. Hri takes her for walks in the morning and I do the evening shift. Grandma takes her for a mid-morning stroll when she visits. We plan our outings around her mealtimes, especially on Sundays, when our helper Rita is off. Thankfully, Rita has taken to Puska and looks after her for the better part of the day, when we are at work. Occasionally, Leia would come over for a playdate.

Puska is so much a part of our family and we all love her so much. She is so attached to us and follows us all around the house. She would have been a really sad dog if she were not allowed into the house. She cocks her ears when we say 'Bye Puska' when we go out, giving us her really sad face, which makes us feel guilty going out. She runs down to greet us when we come home, wagging her happy tail the same way each and every time. Nothing beats being greeted by a happy dog every time we get home.

We do plan our weekends around her and do try to take her out for walks at the Botanic Gardens and for meals with us when we can. I do wish there were more eateries in Singapore that allow dogs!"

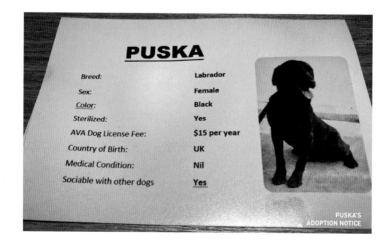

PUSKA

Breed:	Labrador
Sex:	Female
Color:	Black
Sterilized:	Yes
AVA Dog License Fee:	$15 per year
Country of Birth:	UK
Medical Condition:	Nil
Sociable with other dogs	Yes

PUSKA'S ADOPTION NOTICE

> **"**
> Welcoming a dog to the family is a big commitment. Just like children, pee and poo accidents do happen, they can be messy eaters and drinkers, and don't expect your house to be pristine. Just like children, they need their space to run around, they like to play, can be noisy and want attention. But they bring much joy to the family, we love them to bits, and we can't quite imagine life without them.
> **"**

HRI, DILYS, AND SARAH NAIR

#IAdoreMiAmore

Moss was a Narcotics Detector Dog from Singapore Police Force in the K-9 Unit. He met Thaksin during the latter's national service stint in the Singapore Police Force. Thaksin was a narcotic detector dog handler under the Special Operations Command in the K-9 Unit.

"I was enlisted into the Singapore Police Force and I heard about this vocation called the K-9. I was intrigued. Why is there so little information about this unit? Is it as cool as the ones I saw online? Why isn't anyone talking about this unit?

I kept pestering my superior for an opportunity to try out. Tragically, I failed my dog flair test. I begged for a second chance and soon, I found myself standing in front of the kennels with the rest of my batch mates to choose our respective dogs. Amongst the majestic and suave shepards was a black little thing spinning alone in the last kennel. My heart skipped a beat. This little one is so active and adorable. I have never believed in love at first sight until now. I told the batch mates that this doggie is mine!

So many questions raced through my mind. Why is this working dog so cute? Why is he not as fierce as the other dogs in the other kennels? Why is he so adorable? I will be working with him for one and a half years. Will he be co-operative? Can I bring him home? Will I be able to sleep with my working dog, just like in the movies? He looks so playful – will he play me out?

Moss kept spinning in circles and pounced at the kennel door. His eyes were so bright and he was just staring at me, wanting to get out to play.

I was not his first handler. Moss went through several handlers before me. His previous handler had him for a couple of years and they bonded very well. She trained him to be one of the top working dogs in the unit. When I first took him over, I knew that Moss considered me just a replacement. He could never get over his previous handler. Every single time she walked past during his training, he would stop in his tracks and yearn for her.

The two of us would spend at least 10 hours a day together, regularly going to Changi Prison for routine narcotics checks on inmates. Ironically, I have always harboured a MOSS *fear of dogs after being bitten by a canine when I was 14. It was Moss who helped me overcome my fear and bond with her. I loved him so much that I would turn up in camp earlier or stay back after duty to play with him.*

When I completed my National Service, I would contact my juniors back at HQ to ask about him. For three months, all I did was to look at old pictures of Moss. I couldn't bear to be separated from him and asked if I could adopt him after he retired. I really wanted to rehome him and give him the life he deserves after serving the nation so faithfully."

The deal was sealed the minute Moss rushed out of his kennel and pounced excitedly on Mr Thaksin Toh, a full-time national serviceman newly deployed to the police K-9 unit. Mr Toh's heart was won, and the handler and his co-worker, a cocker spaniel, became best friends.

THE STRAITS TIMES
9 JUNE 2017
LEE SI XUAN

Project ADORE is a scheme that allows residents in Housing Board flats to adopt selected medium-sized local mixed breeds that are up to 15kg in weight and 50cm in height. From 2012 till 2017, 562 dogs found homes as a result of this programme.

In 2017, under a one-year pilot expansion co-led by the Ministry of National Development, the Ministry of Home Affairs and the Ministry of Defence, dog handlers from the Singapore Police Force and the Singapore Civil Defence Force who live in HBD flats are now allowed to adopt retired sniffer dogs. Breeds that are permitted include Labrador Retrivers, English Springer Spaniels, Cocker Spaniels and English Pointers.

At the start of June 2017, with the expansion of Project ADORE, Thaksin was finally reunited with his beloved dog. Moss retired at age seven and moved into his new retirement home, Thaksin's 4-room flat in Geylang Bahru.

"It was Madam Eswari, Moss' former trainer, who booked my adoption slot. I had to prove my sincerity to her and assure her that I was committed to take care of him for the rest of his life.

I still remember informing my family that I would be picking Moss up at the Police K-9 headquarters. Everyone was really excited to welcome Moss into our home. The moment he stepped in, he started sniffing around as if he was still on a mission! I laughed and told him, 'It's ok, boy. This is your new home.'

My first day at home with Moss was just blissful. I turned on the air conditioning for him 24/7 because I wanted to spoil him. We now share the same bed every day, his pillow beside mine. I love patting him to sleep. I love to watch him sleep. I love putting my ear close to him and hear him snore. I sometimes feel like Moss is a roommate, sharing the same room and the same bed. Sometime, I see him as my child and I am his pawrent.

I tried to toilet train him, but failed miserably. Until today, he would still avoid the pee tray and instead choose a comfortable spot to relief himself. More often than not (thankfuly), it is near the toilet so all is well.

Moss is a very high energy dog, demanding and very playful. I bring him out for walks twice a day to exercise him and to tire him, to manage his high energy.

I still keep Madam Eswari updated every now and then of Moss' progress with me. She loves hearing stories of him.

Moss has changed my life for the better. I have grown to be more patient; I am happier and I am able to appreciate the little things in life. I have learned to be responsible and gone from someone who used to be afraid of dogs to a devoted dog lover.

I treat him like a king and will continue to do so for the rest of his life. He has brought me great happiness, and I have made his happiness my top priority too."

#Don'tLetThe SunGoDown OnMe

"The first time I met her, for a split second, I thought she was dead. She was lying motionless on a makeshift bed in the corner."

I was with Rachel that faithful evening when she met Oona. We are both volunteers at an animal welfare group and had gathered to send a dog off on her journey to the Rainbow Bridge. Emotions were running high that day. The animal that passed on, an ex-shelter Poodle, was much beloved by the volunteers. As soil was shovelled over her grave, I noticed another hole right next to it. "Another dog is about to go soon", a volunteer whispered softly to me, not wanting to break the solemnity of the evening.

I pieced the story of the other dog together from the bits and bobs of information shared that evening. The shelter had received an urgent appeal in April 2018 from the doggie community requesting that they help with the takeover of two senior dogs, a female Scottish Terrier (named Scottie!) and a male Frenchie. The family could no longer care for them, for reasons best known only to themselves, and were planning to surrender them to the authorities.

Both dogs had a myriad of problems, so despite the passionate appeals by the Animal Welfare Group on social media for potential adopters, not many people expressed interest.

The male Frenchie soon passed on due to his health complications, and the Scottie now lay within a hairs breath of death.

We took a peek at the dog. It was a heartbreaking sight. Her sad, dull, lifeless eyes indicated she had lost the will to live. She had been given a cocktail of intravenous fluids and medication, but lay as still as stone. There was a little debate if she should be sent to the emergency vet. Some were worried that she might give up and die at the clinic if she was admitted overnight.

All of a sudden, the dog lifted her head, as if she understood everything and glanced at Rachel with her soulful eyes. Rachel sprung into action. She cradled the animal in her arms and with the help of another volunteer who drove, rushed her immediately to the clinic. OONA

"I was only hoping she will make it through the night and get better."

Tests and an x-ray were done at the clinic. They discovered that the dog was suffering from a severe infection in her abdominal area. Emergency surgery was recommended and performed. The dog was diagnosed with pancreatic inflammation. She needed lots of rest and recuperation in a safe, quiet environment, and lots of love to cure her broken spirit.

"I had just lost one of my dogs to cancer on 10 October 2018, so I was not prepared to take in another dog, at least not so soon. But I guess it's fate. I knew I would end up bringing her home when she lay on my lap as we made our way to the vet clinic. The only worry I had was how to convince my hubby to agree to me bringing home another dog."

Scottie was discharged after five days of hospitalisation. Rachel's husband, Leslie, accompanied her to the clinic to pick the dog up. She was groggy and walked at a very slow speed because of the discomfort.

"I think this helped in part to convince my hubby fully that she needed a home environment to recover in."

Once home, she was re-named Oona and given a short orientation around the living room. She inspected the area and proceeded to lie flat on the floor to rest. She was extremely well-behaved. It was almost as if she knew she was going to be part of the family so she had to behave and stay clear from trouble.

"The two dogs I was fostering were fine with the newcomer, but my usually dog-friendly foster cat hissed fiercely. Luckily, she accepted Oona's presence in two short days."

Oona slept for the better part of the first day, which was to be expected. The couple took pains to keep her away from the cat whilst she was recovering. Through a mixture of tender loving care, proper medication and the appropriate nutrition, she quickly regained her strength and started to be a little more energetic, joining the pack eagerly at the kitchen entrance during mealtimes.

"We were elated and very proud of her determination to get better. She's a fighter."

Rachel also discovered how fiesty Oona could be when she was babysitting her friend's dog for a fortnight. By then, Oona had become territorial and fiercely protective of the family that rescued her. She started to terrorise any dog who visited. On one occasion, when friends popped by with their doggies for a house party, Oona ended up pinning a miniature pom down with her paws!

As Oona had previously been in a home environment, she had no problems adjusting to Rachel's and Leslie's house. She had no issues walking on leash or using the pee tray.

"She's easygoing and not fussy with food or medications so there were really not many issues."

As she was physically and emotionally weak, Rachel decided not to burden her pet with overtraining.

"I used to teach cute tricks to my first dog. I don't do that any more, especially with my adopted dogs. They have already been through a lot of trauma and I didn't want to stress them further. My only hope is for them to be healthy and happy."

For a dog that was literally knocking on death's door, Oona has made a most miraculous recovery. She may be almost blind, which could account for her chilli-padi feistiness, a coping mechanism to defend herself, but she is a loyal loving dog to her new family. She has unconditionally accepted Rachel and Leslie as her pawrents, whilst being an absolute terror to other dogs who dare to wander onto her turf.

"Oona's adoption was most unexpected, but I would like to think that my late dog, Leilei, had a part to play in this. I had just lost her (on the 10 Oct 2018), a few days before I met Oona and I was struck by how similar both their stories were. I brought Leilei home back in 2014 because she was in critical condition. The same for Oona. If I had met Oona when she's healthy, I would probably not have adopted her."

She has definitely helped my hubby and I in healing emotionally after the loss of Leilei. My hubby spent two weeks sleeping with Oona every night in one room while I slept with my friend's dog and the fosters in another room. She now follows my hubby around the house like his little bodyguard."

A responsible dog owner needs to have lots of patience and love and be committed to caring for their dog till the end of its life. They need to make the effort in providing the best care for their dogs.

"I will be very sad when that day comes, but I know I'll have to move on. We spend a lot of time cuddling her and telling her we love her. We are not sure how attached she was with her previous family, but I hope she feels more love now than ever before."

Rachel and Leslie went above and beyond their call of duty, and saved not just another shelter dog but snatched this one from the clutches of the doggie grim reaper. No one knows how many more years this eleven-year-old Scottish Terrier will have, but she will definitely live out the rest of her days in a comfortable home surrounded by a most loving family.

> **“**
>
> I got my first dog from a pet store in January 2006 when she was two months old. When she was diagnosed with nasal cancer at seven years old, I was devastated. My hubby and I spent all our savings on various treatments but the illness took away her life after six months. I then went on to volunteer in animal shelters. From there, I learnt more about stray and abandoned animals and the condition of breeding dogs at puppy mills. Since then, I have been adopting and fostering retired breeding dogs. While you may prefer those cute puppies in the pet stores, there are many dogs at the animal shelters waiting for their forever home. Do give them a chance and consider them. Adopt, don't shop.
>
> **”**
>
> RACHEL AND LESLIE

#TheGoldenGirl

"In August 2013, I went down to the adoption drive again. Ginny was still there. I stayed for four hours, just watching. No one showed any interest in her at all, but I was too afraid to register mine.

Over three consecutive years, I visited numerous adoption drives but I knew I was not ready for another dog. I was scared of getting hurt, too afraid that the dog would pass on too quickly after the adoption. I was absolutely devastated when two of my aged dogs passed on in 2010 and 2011, four months apart and I wasn't sure if I could live through that again. Then someone mentioned that even if these rescues were to live for only three months, at least they would have experienced three months of love in a warm, cosy home that they never had."

Eleanor is a volunteer at the shelter which I adopted Leia from, and mom to four children – her son Russ and her three furkids, Lily, Rosie and Ginny. Her many years of experience caring for shelter dogs, especially with an adopted special needs pup of her own, meant that she quickly became part of my doggie support system when I welcomed Leia into my home. Her knowledge of shelter dog behaviour and health issues, as well as tips on how to slowly integrate ex-breeding dogs into the normal world, proved to be invaluable for me as a first time adopter.

Part of her knowledge came from her first hand experience with her adopted girl, Ginny. Ginny was an ex-breeding dog who was rescued by the Animal Welfare Group. She was placed in a foster home for a few months before she was transferred to the shelter.

Eleanor first laid eyes on Ginny in June of 2013. By then, she had been visiting their adoption drive religiously for about six months. She was always tempted to take one of the dogs home, but she wasn't ready. She had a soft spot for ex-breeding dogs and wanted to do as much as she could to help them. That faithful day, she had visited the shelter to drop off some beds and bags for their fund-raising activities.

"There at the corner of a cage, I saw Ginny. She looked extremely timid, probably because she only had one eye (her other eyeball is embedded in her cheek, the result – I'm assuming – of rough handling at the puppy mill). My instant thought was to take her home immediately, but I wasn't sure if I was ready to welcome another dog into my life, especially after the recent loss of my two beloved dogs in quick succession. I thought about her constantly and found myself fretting if she had been adopted by someone else. I felt such a strong connection with her even though my introduction to her was fleeting. I questioned myself if I was indeed ready for another dog.

GINNY

I saw a lady pick Ginny out and was pleased that someone was willing to give this imperfect dog a chance, but my heart sank when she started to examine her. I knew in my heart that dog a chance, but my heart sank when she started to examine her. I knew in my heart that she would not follow through with the adoption. True enough, Ginny was returned to the pen. I stepped forward and asked the volunteer if I could take a closer look at the dog. That's when I knew I was ready.

FIRST DAY

FIRST WEEK

> 66
>
> Adopt! Adopt! Adopt!
> If you need to purchase, do not buy from pet stores. All puppies sold there are from puppy mills. Even if you think you have found a responsible breeder, do your homework thoroughly. They could be greedy mills using one or two former champions to justify the exhorbitant price of a pup, bred usually under horrific, inhumane conditions.
>
> 99

ELEANOR TAN

Everything happened really quickly. I was asked to proceed to the registration counter to fill up a form. A screener from the main team spoke with me to find out if I had the means to cope with an ex-breeding dog. Some people may find this process intrusive and unnecessary but I was grateful to have had this conversation so I could better understand the special needs of former puppy mill dogs because of their traumatic past lives. Many of these dogs have never experience real life, having been confined in a tiny cage all their lives. They also ensured that I understood the emotional commitment and financial responsibilities that came with the adoption. I was impressed that the shelter volunteers took the pains to ensure the dogs end up in the right homes and go to families that will care for them for the rest of their lives.

Before I knew it, Ginny was on the way home with me. She sat quietly on my lap, shivering the whole way.

When we got to the house, I carried her to the kitchen to get her to drink. She just sat there, frozen to the spot. She was nervous so I let her be. I put a comfy mat on the floor and placed her on it. She slept right through the first night.

My dog Bubbles was already 13 when Ginny joined the household so she was very chilled and accommodating of the new dog from word go.

The next couple of months were very tiring for me. Ginny suffered from very bad sarcoptic mange and had to be confined for almost two months. My late Bichons never had any health issues, so it was a little challenging initially. As the condition was zoonotic* and highly contagious, I had to confine her and clean the space thoroughly twice a day. I spent as much time as I could afford with her in the confinement space, keeping her company and reassuring her that she was safe. Ginny was such a trooper. Never once did she complain.

Training was not at the top of my list. I knew I was dealing with an animal that had experienced so much stress in her life, a dog who was not equipped for life in the outside world, so I knew I had to be

extremely patient and accommodating with her. I did not (and would never) force Ginny to do anything she's not comfortable with. She hated the collar and leash so I would carry her whenever we are out. Toilet training was not important to me too. Ex-breeding dogs live, breathe and defecate in their cage 24/7, and it would be very stressful to her if I were to force toilet training upon her at this late stage in her life. So I let her learn at her own pace.

My only goal was to ensure her happiness.

Ginny is a very easy, laid back dog. She doesn't move about much and is happiest just lying on her favourite mat. She only wakes to walk to the kitchen to drink or to ease herself. And, very occasionally, she would emerge to play with the other dogs.

Ginny is a very different dog today and has absolute trust in me! From a timid girl who used to shun humans, she has learned that not all humans are cruel. She will happily welcome guests to the house and flip over to demand belly rubs. I have learned so much from her. She has taught me patience and I have gained a wealth of knowledge on canine health just dealing with her issues.

Ginny is very precious to me and I bend over backwards to make sure she has a good life, but I am careful not to humanise her. I am very protective of her but I try my best not to let her lose her sense of dog. I feel for the dogs whose owners manifest their love by spoonfeeding them to keep their fur clean, overdress them in human clothes, push them around in a pram so that they don't get their paws dirty and overfeed them because a fat dog is a happy dog. Overweight dogs suffer from a host of health issues and places unnecessary stress on their legs.

I only succumbed to the pram when I was traumatised by an incident in a car park in 2016. By then, Ginny had acquired a new sister, Lily. I had leashed up the dogs but decided to carry all three. Ginny couldn't walk, young Lily was tugging and senior Bubbles was being dragged along by her. After a few steps, Ginny slipped out of my arms and fell to the floor. I was horrified. Thankfully, she was ok.

*zoonotic: a disease that normally exists in animals but can infect/be transmitted to humans.

I somehow managed to hang on to the leashes of the other two dogs. Lesson learnt! There's a time and place for doggie prams, and this was it. Ginny is my fourth dog. Some time after I adopted her, Bubbles passed on, and I got two other dogs to keep her company. Apart from Ginny, all my other dogs were either given to me or purchased from ethical breeders.

In 1996, I got my first dog, a Bichon. A good friend was a registered and ethical Bichon breeder. I fostered her whilst she competed in conformation shows* (a common practice in the show scene). All my friend wanted in return was a litter from her, after studying her lines and examining her health records. After her show career ended, she was officially mine. I acquired my second Bichon in the same way.

From that first dog till now, with the exception of Ginny, I've only always had Bichons. I am extremely passionate and knowledgable about the breed. Having also had experience in the show circuit, I know what a 'proper' Bichon should look like and what the right temperament is. I have also done extensive research on the ethical and responsible breeding of Bichons, and have been in the loop with the reputable breeders in the show scene. These are breeders who do so for the betterment of the breed. I have learnt so much from them and I understand what responsible breeding is.

Because of my research, I also know the horrors of puppy mills. I have abhorred them ever since. In the late nineties, I tried to get as much information as possible about them and even paid a visit to a few of them. The few dogs I saw in there were in a pathetic state. I made up my mind that I would one day rescue a puppy mill survivor.

To everyone who has asked me for advice on purchasing a designer offspring from an award-winning dog, I would advise them to do their homework and not take everything they are told at face value. Many puppy mills operate under the

veneer of ethical breeding because people are uninformed and do not do their due research. Interested owners should find out everything about the breeders, ask them lots of questions and follow them through the dog show circuit. A good breeder will answer all your questions without excuses and, in return, have a plethora of questions for you too. They will also allow you to see the parents of the puppies.

A good breeder would have the health of both doggie parents tested thoroughly before breeding. They would arrange for a hip and an ophthalmologist evaluation and ensure that the dog is free from genetic defects. The temperament and characteristics that typifies a standard Bichon must also be taken into consideration as well. The breeder should have a contract for the potential buyer with strict terms that include no breeding and the necessity to sterilise. Most good breeders will also do a house check before they release a pup.

My son and I started volunteering at the shelter after I adopted Ginny. Saving puppy mill survivors is a cause I believe strongly in, and I do as much as I can to help these dogs. I have also lobbied hard to try to change people's perception of rescue dogs as aggressive, filthy and ugly. Many people believe shelter dogs, being older, are never able to form a bond with their owner. Many of them are timid and insecure with trust issues in humans, but these are problems that can easily be solved with love and patience. Many of the volunteers and I form a support system for all new adopters so that they have someone they can turn to for advice.

My son has been exposed to dogs of all sizes and temperaments from a very young age, and grew up learning to love and respect them. As he was growing up, I was always by his side, advising him on the rights and wrongs of how to handle dogs. I believe many accidents happen because the parents are not there to teach their children the proper way to handle dogs, and unfortunately, regardless of whose fault it is, the dogs are always at the losing end. Russ has always loved all dogs unconditionally and throws himself into volunteer work enthusiastically. He has ambitions to pursue a veterinary degree, with my wholehearted support.

*A conformation show is a breed show in which a judge familiar with a specific dog breed evaluates purebred dogs for how well they conform to the established breed type as described in the individual breed's standard.

SHAVED BY THE VET

SHAVED BY THE VET

BIRTHDAY WITH
HER SISTERS

Russ has always been very close to all my dogs, and stayed with all my senior dogs till the very end. Losing a dog is very painful and he was totally devastated each time. The indescribable pain left him a total wreak when my first had to be put down after she suffered a stroke when she was 15, followed four months later by the death of my second from a heart attack. Bubbles passed on at 17 after battling kidney disease for two and a half years. He and I still miss them tremendously. The pain never goes away, even if we try to focus our love on our present furkids. Russ is as protective of Ginny as I, guiding her gently to the toilet or the kitchen if she is disorientated.

On 6 November 2018, Ginny did not go to the kitchen when I called the dogs together for lunch. She looked dazed and stared blankly into space. I tested her by moving my palm suddenly towards her face. There was no reaction. I realised she could be completely blind. Concerned at how sudden the blindness struck, I brought her to the vet the following day for a full check and blood tests. Diabetes was ruled out. It was suspected to be because of a matured cataract.

Ginny was quick to bounce back on track. She still managed to navigate her way around the house. She was only spooked by the sound of kibbles against her metal bowl so I spread the kibbles on the floor and pushed them towards her as she ate. It worked. I also feed the dogs rehydrated raw food, which is softer. She seems not to have lost her appetite along with her eyesight, and we try to help her maintain the same quality of life before the blindness.

Lily and Rosie have been very considerate. They would guide Ginny through the kitchen door if she was unsure if the glass door was opened. They avoid rough play and have stopped trying to annoy her. They know better than to mess around with the old lady!

Our dogs may have much shorter lives than us, but as long as they are with us, we should care for them, love them and do the best for them till their very last breath. We love them dearly and treasure every single second we spend with them."

#PetShopBoys

"Sometimes, the ones we rescue, rescue us instead."

In the spring of 2018, I collaborated with Terry Peh on a doggie runway show. It was a massive production with more than 20 dogs and an equal number of dog-loving fashion models, celebrities and personalities all coming together to advocate Responsible Dog Ownership.

Terry is wildly passionate about promoting the importance of adoption, and the repercussion of buying your dogs. So I was completely taken aback when he told me his first dog, Toby, was purchased from a pet shop. Ironically, that experience proved so challenging that he decided to go the adoption route the second time around.

"It was a Sunday morning in 2008 when I stepped into a pet shop along Upper Thomson Road. Toby was just 3 months old. He had a dark coat and looked roguishly scruffy. He circled around the crate excitedly and looked at me intensely with his soulful eyes, as if he knew he was going home with me.

TOBY RUSS

Cradling a warm, cuddly puppy in my arms and carrying him home was an incredible feeling. I was literally on cloud nine but the happiness was short lived. To my horror I spotted several red spots and bald patches on his body. I turned to my good friend Google for help. My heart sank when I realised they were ringworms.

I returned to the shop and confronted the owner (lets call him G) who said he would take Toby back and I could bring another dog home with me. I declined his offer and asked if the pet shop could send him to a vet. I would return to get Toby when he was nursed back to health. G replied that it was against company policy – the only resolution he could offer was to exchange the "defective product" with a new one. 'What was going to happen to Toby then?' I asked. He kept silent.

It struck me immediately that Toby (and all the other animals in the shop) were treated like disposable products, to be discarded like rubbish if found defective. The owner of the pet shop essentially did not care and wasn't going to help Toby get better. I realised that, by purchasing from him, I was contributing to the demand for puppies, fueling their supply from puppy mills, and supporting pet shops with erroneous business practices like G's. Social media was still at its infancy in 2008, and there was a general lack of awareness and education about puppy mills and dog adoption. I learnt it all the hard way."

Terry was determined to do his best for Toby. It took him almost 18 months before his skin condition got better. Those eighteen months proved to be a crazy roller coaster ride for him.

"I had to shave him down. He was bare for eight months while he was being treated. I even contracted ringworms from him and had to clean my entire house with bleach. But I loved him and never gave up on him. After all, the family that itches together, stays together!"

When it was about time to get a second dog, Terry decided to adopt. He stumbled upon an ad on Gumtree placed by a couple. The official reason given was a downsizing of lodging, and unfortunately, the tiny schnauzer did not feature in any of their future plans.

Russ was described as healthy and well-trained. He looked bright and cheery in the picture, and Terry was drawn to him.

"It was a no brainer so I picked Russ up and took him back for a two-week home trial. Meeting Russ was akin to being catfished on Tinder. His long, matted fur was unruly and reeked of urine. He was extremely obese and had a rapid tremor in his front legs. He was in a really bad shape.

Russ had a lot of baggage. He had severe anxiety issues, he barked excessively, he was not toilet-trained and he chewed on furniture. I would come back to a soiled home after a long day at work. Our place was in a constant mess and the neighbours were complaining about the incessant barking. I brought in a trainer but the situation did not improve. Once again, we were not prepared for the task and it took a lot of time, effort and investment to help Russ slowly adjust to his new home."

By some strange co-incidence, Terry discovered (when his ex-owners handed over the balance of his grooming credits) that Russ had also been purchased from the same pet shop as Toby!

When Russ first met Toby for the first time, he was submissive. But he soon got comfortable in the house and started competing with the younger dog. He would drink out of Toby's bowl and steal his toys. And compete for attention and affection.

"He knew what he was doing and was clearly testing boundaries. Russ and Toby together were like Pinky and the Brain. It was a lot of fun to watch but I also knew (my wife and) I would have to put in a lot of hard work if he was to stay."

Toby came at a time when Terry lost his mum to cancer.

"My relationship with Dad had always been less than ideal so the addition of Toby brought some joy to the family and helped us tide over a difficult time. Toby also brought Dad and I closer and our relationship improved tremendously. I guess dogs can magically help break the ice and warm our hearts in their own wonderful ways."

That joy was short lived, however. Terry's decision to adopt Russ wasn't made in consultation with the family because he had assumed there would be no issues.

"I did not expect Russ to come with (so much) baggage. It came to a point where I had to consider giving Russ up because my relationship with Dad had deteriorated so much due to my dog's poor potty behaviour and incessant barking. Coming home became a stressful affair. I knew I had to make a choice between Dad and Russ.

One night I plucked up my courage, packed what I needed, picked the two boys up and left home without a word. That was one of the best decisions I've ever made.

I realised Russ had a problem and he needed me to help plug the gap. Giving him up was as good as passing on the problem to someone else. And that was not only irresponsible but also extremely unfair (and stressful) to Russ. There was also the very real possibility of him ending up in a shelter, and eventually euthanised. I could not let that happen to him."

Distance also proved to make the heart fonder.

"When I left home with the boys, I thought Dad and I would not ever talk again and reconcile our problems. But it was actually that little distance and space that allowed us to re-evaluate our relationship – and when we reconnected, we came from a place of empathy and love, rather than selfishness and resentment. All thanks to my dogs"

> ❝
> Every day, countless dogs are robbed of their rights to live or access to basic care. Raising rescued dogs comes with it's own set of struggles, something which not many adopters are willing to talk about. This inspired me to set up Good Dog People, to empower the community to count more meaningful memories with their dogs – through responsible products, vet-authored resources and partnerships with social enterprises.
> ❞

TERRY PEH

(L-R)
TOBY, RUSS

When Terry started raising Toby and Russ, he realised there was little regulation in the commercial pet food market.

"You can't be sure that what you're feeding your pets is quality food, despite the claims the packaging may make. When you scrutinise the ingredients' list, you find a lot of these claims to be inflated, and some of these ingredients are actually bad for your dogs."

66

What is a responsible dog owner?

Living in a densely populated and multi-racial city like Singapore, we ought to be more aware and sensitive of every individual's acceptance towards dogs.

Basic etiquette like picking up after your dog(s); being aware of theo public common spaces that are or are not pet-friendly; leashing your dogs outdoor at all times, to name but a few. These are all just basic manners.

Being responsible for the safety of your dogs is of utmost importance and should be prioritised at all costs.

Investing in behavioural training amidst a busy working schedule can be hard but it is so important. It is almost non-negotiable if we want our dogs to live harmoniously with our neighbours in the hood.

Raising a dog may not be easy but their unconditional love, and the joy they bring will make it all worthwhile.

99

TERRY PEH

Besides the obvious lack of regulations, he realised that (like himself), there were lots of people out there who faced the challenges of being a first time dog owner. These were people who might have had bad experiences with pet shops subscribing to poor ethics; a new dog adopter who had no idea how to induct an abandoned dog with baggage; a dog owner who was inundated with so much noise on the net regarding health issues and needed some clarity.

He quit his job to start GoodDogPeople, an on-line store that retails a carefully curated inventory of quality doggie products.

Toby and Russ have grown into doggie middle age comfortably under the loving care of Terry and Wenxin. But the past still continues to haunt the older dog.

RUSS WHEN HE WAS ADOPTED

TOBY AT THE PET SHOP

"Russ' continued insecurity stems from his past experience as an abandoned pet. He is always craving for attention which never seems to be enough. I learnt from his ex-owner that he was never allowed into the house because the elders did not like the idea of having a dog in the living space. So Russ lived his first two years in an outdoor kennel at their front yard. I always wonder why they got a dog in the first place.

When he first came into our home, he was very sensitive to being grabbed by the legs, which fortunately got better after many years of conditioning. His incessant barking due to anxiety went on for many years and recently relapsed after we put Tilda (another rescue) on home trial for few days.

It's clear to me that these traumas inflicted on mistreated and abandoned dogs stay with them for life."

As for the infamous 'G', his shop is still trading. A quick online search would reveal several similar negative experiences from other customers.

"Consumers fuel the growth of such businesses by buying into their lies (e.g. "healthy" puppies from responsible breeders). I even read on the net that there are businesses that are even dishonest with mark downs (e.g. scrubbing and reprinting food expiry dates to resell). The only way to stop these businesses is to report, do more research and demand more transparency."

Knowledge is power, and it may help save your pet's life one day.

"The recent laws from California and the UK are paving the way for policy makers worldwide (including Singapore) to put more vested interest in improving animal welfare. But this is not the end of our fight. Enforcing compliance on pet stores is just scratching the surface. We must look at the entire supply chain, from breeding to consumption. Stricter enforcement on licensed breeders and heavier penalties on private breeders are necessary. There should also be continued education for consumers and pet business owners as demand of pure breeds will definitely fuel the black market.

As pet ownership increases rapidly worldwide, problems contributed by puppy mills and pet abandonment will become more glaring in time to come. Every conversation is an opportunity to educate and we must know that whilst the policy makers will accelerate progress, every individual is empowered to influence and educate any new or existing dog owners.

It starts with you and me."

SHOT ON LOCATION

ODE TO ART GALLERY

66

Don't let the attitudes of others get you down. Concentrate on you and your dog.

99

JAY GURDEN
dogstodaymagazine.co.uk

> When people tell me they want to give up a senior, I don't even ask why anymore. I just assume that the people have an attachment disorder or basically they are selfish and have no heart. We need to stop asking what the dog did and ask what the owner didn't do. Training, vetting, love. People ruin animals and kids but both can be healed.

REMEMBER ME RESCUE NY

66

*And in the end,
it's not the years in your life
that count; It's the life in
your years.*

99

ABRAHAM LINCOLN

#SheWorksHard ForTheMoney

"Dogs need love, dogs need a home and dogs need our help. I will do my very best to help them If it is within my means to do so. It really is not that difficult a concept to understand."

AA was an eight-year-old ex-breeding dog formerly known as Dachses when Dollei first set eyes on her.

"I got to know of her existence because, I'm ashamed to admit, one of my friends is a breeder."

According to the RSPCA website, breeding dogs are victims of the high-volume puppy industry. They are bred for profit and kept in tiny, filthy cages. These dogs don't receive any affection, exercise or proper veterinary care. And when they can no longer produce puppies, they are discarded.

In order to maximise profit, commercial breeders want to produce the highest number of puppies at the lowest possible cost. Breeding dogs are kept in tiny cages, because more adult dogs to breed equals more puppies, which equals more money. Cruel breeders maximize space by keeping mother and father dogs tightly contained, often in ramshackle outdoor pens, exposed to the elements, or in tiny, filthy cages for their entire lives. Caged dogs develop lesions and sores from constantly standing on uncomfortable wire flooring, and often get injured by the wire's sharp points. Dogs of all ages and sizes may be crammed in together, which can lead to stress, aggression and fighting. Because the cages are usually stacked vertically, urine and feces rain down onto the dogs below. They aren't taken on walks, and don't get to play with toys or run around. They eat, sleep, relieve themselves and give birth in these cages.

Since breeding dogs aren't seen by the public, they aren't bathed and their hair is not brushed or cut. These dogs are left to suffer through painful injuries, broken bones, rotting teeth, dangerous levels of filth, festering mats that pull at their skin, and nails so long that they curl back into and pierce their paw pads.

As health care is costly, breeding dogs in nasty breeding facilities have poor access to veterinary care and hygiene. They are not typically cared for by a veterinarian, not vaccinated, they do not go for regular checkups, not even when they're sick and they are never sent for teeth cleaning.

> "
> I think a responsible dog owner is attentive to their dog's needs. They ensure their dogs are getting the right food and the right diet for their breed, size and health. Dogs rely on us for almost everything and they are the ones who suffer for our negligence. Health is a priority. So is grooming and keeping them clean and disease-free.
> "
>
> DOLLEI SEAH

The filthy conditions encourage the spread of diseases, especially amongst puppies with immature immune systems. Sometimes, these illnesses can be life-threatening, painful and expensive to treat. Puppies often arrive in pet stores with health issues ranging from parasites to parvo to pneumonia. Because puppies are removed from their mothers at a very young age, they can also suffer from fear, anxiety and other lasting behavioural problems. Because quality is not a priority for cruel breeders, they don't bother to remove medically compromised dogs from their breeding stock, resulting in generation after generation of dogs with unchecked hereditary defects. These frequently include heart disease, deafness, bone disorders like hip dysplasia, and blood and respiratory disorders. Sometimes, these issues don't show up until people bring the puppy home, only to be confronted with unpredictable, expensive and oftentimes chronic medical problems.

Female dogs are treated like puppy-making machines. They are bred at every opportunity, without any rest time between litters, and when their bodies are so depleted that they can no longer produce puppies, they're often abandoned or killed. Their only job is to produce puppies for as long as they live.

That's the cruel reality of breeding dogs.

"I would show up randomly to check on the dogs and nag him to give up this cruel, heartless business. I always threatened to report him to the authorities if I saw any signs of mistreatment, and that has kept him on his toes. But I was never allowed into the back room so I guessed that there were parts of the mill that hid terrible horrors."

She first met Dachses on one of these random visits.

"She was pregnant when I saw her. Our eyes met and I immediately felt a special connection with her. A chill ran through my body, and images of my late dog MeiMei suddenly flashed through my mind.

MeiMei was a mixed breed street dog whom I had adopted from SPCA. I lost her when I brought her to the vet for scaling. She was given an overdose of GA and never woke up from the procedure. I never ever forgave myself for that."

Dachses had the exact same vibe as MeiMei. She even looked at Dollei in the same way. It was almost as if she was a reincarnation of her late dog.

Dollei harressed her breeder friend, who told her eventually ("to get me off his back!") that he would allow her to adopt the dog in a few years (when he had milked enough of the animal for his own use). So Dollei waited patiently. She asked about the dog constantly, and prayed hard for her safety. That was really all she could do whilst waiting.

"Before I brought Dachses home, I spoke with QQ, my rescued mongrel (via an animal communicator). My other rescue, Osha, had passed away and QQ was all alone. I told her that I was going to bring AA home, to prepare her for it."

Dachses reached her retirement age and the breeder was ready to release her. The day finally came for Dollei to pick the dog up.

"Unfortunately, I was travelling when I got the call to let me know she's ready for adoption. I could not fly home in time so I told them to hold on to her till I got home.

Shortly, I got another message from them informing me that she is in heat and they've mated her! I immediately arranged for a friend to get her out, but they refused to release her, as they had to confirm if she was pregnant.

I prayed and prayed really hard but it was not to be. She was pregnant, so they kept her till she gave birth to what would be her last batch of puppies. Sadly, only one amongst the three survived."

Dachses was with her surviving baby when Dollei arrived to take her.

"I had to separate the mother from her son. She was breastfeeding him then.

I took a deep breath, went to the cage, opened the door, held AA tight and told her to come with me. She was so nervous, she peed. She was shaking all over and refused to move.

Her baby was jumping all around her, whining and refusing to leave the mother.

I did not have a choice, I knew I had to leave immediately or risk the breeder changing his mind. I could not fathom the thought of AA continuing to live and breed in the appalling conditions. Their concern was not for the mother but the son. He would be sold for a tidy profit and would soon be in a home.

I grabbed AA tight in my arms. The baby started screaming and she began to struggle. I held her close to my heart and promised her I would be a responsibe owner and love her till the end.

We could hear her son barking and whinning louder and louder.

> **66**
> I thought I rescued her but, on hindsight, it was the reverse. She has brought the family so much closer together. Everyone wants a part of her. They miss her as soon as they leave my house, so her neediness has gotten me a lot of attention too!
> **99**

DOLLEI SEAH

135

She looked totally lost. She kept looking back. And suddenly, she stared into my eyes. I stopped and broke down.

I asked for the baby but they refused to release him to me. And I could not afford to pay what the pet shop would be willing to fork out for him.

I had to save the mother.

I knew we could not turn back, so I continued to walk as fast as I could and jumped straight into the car. I kept apologising to her for taking her away from her baby."

When Dollei got home, AA was so scared she had no idea what to do. She had never been in a home before and everything looked and felt alien to her.

"She was mentally and physically paralysed for more than a week. She refused to move, refused to eat, refused to drink. My entire family came over every day to keep her company. To speak with her, massage her, comfort her, to make her feel safe and wanted.

We realised she did not know how to lie down and sleep properly, probably because she had been locked in a tiny cage her whole life.

It was amazing how gentle and protective QQ was towards her. QQ is known to be very unpredictable, with an aggressive temperament, especially with other dogs. I was so afraid she might snap at AA. But, on the contrary, she was super gentle towards the smaller dog. They got along so well. Imagine the 29kg QQ and the malnourished 4.6kg AA cuddling together!"

To help AA assimilate into the household, Dollei allowed her to choose her safe spot, a quiet corner of the house, and left her there. She was allowed her to venture out at her own time, when she was ready.

She was slowly introduced to normal things like toys and soft beds, but it was never forced upon her. Teaching her tricks was the absolute last thing on their agenda.

Medical care was of the utmost importance. She was brought to the vet as soon as she settled down. She was treated for heartworm, had eight of her teeth extracted and an 8cm tumor removed at another session.

"Toilet training was crazy but I totally understood why she didn't grasp the concept. Since she was born, she had eaten, slept and defecated in the same place, so the idea of having designated places for each activity was completely foreign to her. So I just let her be. As time passed, she learnt to use the pee pad, but accidents still continue to happen. I let it pass. I'm just happy that she is happy and healthy. We have learnt to watch for the signs, and to be faster than her to clean up her shit so she doesn't soil the entire house!!!!

AA is the fourth dog I've adopted and the first from a breeding farm. My first dog, Ossa, was rescued from a factory when she was about two months old. The Indian workers there were trying to catch and eat her! Ozzy, the dog that passed away because of the negligence of a vet, was adopted from SPCA at four months, and my current furkid, QQ, was abandoned at the neighbourhood temple along with her bed, her toys and her leash when she was two months old.

AA is a dog that is filled with love. She would cuddle up and give her love to everyone, and loved to be near people. She has a special gift of calming even the most agitated person down. That, to me, is truly magical.

I love all my dogs unconditionally. Each and every day with them is a gift. Everything about them is wonderful.

I will never ever give up on them. Because your dog will never give up on you."

#What'sLove GotToDoWithIt

"Pluto cannot make the shoot, I'm sorry. I can't risk a seizure attack if he gets excited." his owner Shu Hui texted.

When I was understudying to be an AWG (animal welfare group) volunteer, one of the most important lessons I learnt was the strict screening process of potential adopters.

Whilst shelters depend on the generousity, kindness and empathy of dog lovers to give their rescues a good home, it is also absolutely imperative that they weed out the wheat from the chaff in order to separate the gems from the garbage.

Some people attend adoption drives because they think it's a convenient source of free dogs or basement bargain pedigree finds. There are others who treat them as a one-stop-shop doggie supermarket. And there are some who are there to pick up a dog as a surprise present like it was an inanimate stuffed toy.

Landing in the wrong house can sometimes be deadly for the dog.

There was the case of a new adopter who flouted the rules and let her newly adopted pooch off-leash barely a week after bringing her home, only to lose the panicked dog near a busy road filled with heavy traffic. She was tragically hit by a car and killed. A new pawrent disposed of his beloved poodle in a black trash bag, chucked unceremoniously 10 metres away in a corner of their common corridor far from the house. And the story of a family who was seen happily purchasing a new puppy a week after their adopted dog perished under mysterious circumstances.

So, whilst it is indeed a joyful occasion when a dog finds a great home, it is also a cause of tremendous stress and concern for both volunteer and dog when they get placed in the hands of a totally irresponsible or unsuitable adopter.

PLUTO

Some people, are just not cut out for doggie tinder. They get upset and abusive when volunteers do not swipe left on their applications. Others, when told they are not ready for a pet, march off in a huff to the nearest pet shop to purchase a puppy instead, in some form of misguided protest. Ultimately, the dogs lose out. Some of these pups get abandoned, surrendered to the authorities to be euthanised or thrown by the wayside when the owners have grown tired of their novelty.

Shu Hui, a senior volunteer at an AWG, recalled rejecting a couple, self-professed dog lovers who wanted to adopt a pug. They came across as the sort of owners who wanted a specific breed purely for aesthetic reasons but without the knowledge to care for it or the problems that come with it.

The problem is even more pressing now, as dogs are genetically altered to meet certain aesthetic demands. According to an article in *The Guardian*, dated 5 April 2016, the growing popularity of dogs with extremely wide faces and short bodies like bulldogs and pugs, fuelled in part by celebrity fads and trends, have prompted canine experts to put out warnings of health related issues associated with these breeds. The inherent body shape of these dogs is high risk for many different disorders like breathing difficulties, skin disorders, overheating, eye conditions and premature death.

Professor Paul McGreevy, a research author from the University of Sydney also believes that "... people need to think very seriously about what drives the decisions they are making. They should really reflect on what they are actually investing in and committing to."

Shelter dogs come with their own unique set of challenges, problems which can be further differentiated into categories like street rescues, abused, neglected or ex-breeding dogs. Each have their own peculiar idiosyncracies and unique habits, which would take a very special patient, kind, generous adopter to overcome. The dogs might never have seen the light of day, having been cooped up in a cage all their lives. They may be skittish cos of previous abusive experiences. They may have severe health problems resulting from neglect or poor nutrition. Screening not only allows the volunteers to determine if the potential adopter is ready to face these challenges but to also paint that picture to the would-be doggie pawrent.

However, Pluto's potential owners did not seem to be too clued in, nor did they seem willing to invest time and effort in learning and caring for the dog. They claimed to have some experience with dogs, but not pugs, which they wanted cos they said it was a cute breed.

Shu Hui explained to them why they were not quite ready at the moment, but instead of engaging in conversation to learn how to prepare themselves, they stormed out angrily to the puppy mill next door to purchase their designer pug of noble bloodlines.

Fast forward a few months and the shelter received a message on their Facebook page. The writer had a pug which he wanted to give up for adoption. He sounded desperate.

Unfortunately, at that time, the shelter had a kennel cough epidemic so it wasn't a good time for new dogs to be brought there. However, something about the message didn't sound right and the guy sounded desperately urgent to give him up immediately. Not wanting to risk anything untoward happening to the dog should she procrastinate, Shu Hui contacted the guy to get the dog from him immediately.

It was the same guy she had rejected at the adoption drive.

"I'm sure it was fate that brought us together. It was a weekday night and all the other volunteers were busy. I was the only one available for the rescue!"

Just before she picked the pug up, the ex-owner told Shu Hui that his dog was possessed. He would cry in the middle of the night; he kept walking in circles, didn't know how to pee in the toilet and was impossible to train. He was just not the ideal pug that they thought he would be.

He lied that he had adopted Pluto from somewhere else but was able to provide his exact birth date! (1 July 2016). He obviously did not remember the incident at the adoption drive.

The previous owners could not wait to get rid of their dog. Shu Hui remember him messaging her non-stop, asking me when I am going to collect him. They did not even have any pics of Pluto to send over. That was how much they loved him.

Pluto was picked up on 24th April 2018.

"I was disappointed with the couple. I knew something was wrong with the dog from the way he behaved, and his owners were just so conveniently giving up on him without even trying to help this poor little guy."

The moment she saw him, she knew he had to go to a home to rest instead of going to the shelter. It's always a struggle to decide which dog to prioritize. But Pluto's medical problems seemed serious and not many families would be able to cope with his condition.

"After we left that house, I let him walk on the grass patch and he started to wobble and walk in circles. He had no idea where he is going. He was also panting heavily non-stop. When I brought him home and saw him walking into walls, I realised that he was partially blind. "

For a young, two-year old pug, Pluto seemed to have a lot of frequent seizures. Shu Hui consulted several vets. The first suspected it was Cushings disease. The second diagnosed it as Pug Dog Encephalitis (PDE), a rare genetic pug disorder which causes a lot of neuro issues. According to the vet, this was a result of being badly bred.

Truth be told, Shu Hui was not ready to foster any dogs at that point in time, "but after witnessing his first seizure, my heart broke and just want to ensure that he is safe in a home."

But first, she had to make sure she had the time, finances and support system needed to care for him. His illness is incurable. Eventually, if his kidneys and liver fail, he might have to be put to sleep. She had to be mentally prepared for that day too.

"I can never forget the first time his vet told me he has PDE. The seizures will be constant and frequent and only steroids can keep his condition under control. My heart breaks every time he has an attack. They last for up to 10 minutes each time. He will scream in pain and lose control of his bowels. It's so painful to watch but I have to be there for him, to administer the medication to make the seizure stop. He needs someone to carry him whenever his seizure kicks in, if not he will start banging his head on the wall and against the floor, wailing out loud and crying in pain. It's like watching a kid suffer and yet, there is only limited help I can give."

Pluto has to be medicated at least twice a day. Since he is very food motivated, it is quite easy to mix tablets into his meals. However, the medication is costly and has to be administered for life. The dosages will increase over time. There are the numerous blood tests and vet reviews every other month to consider. Shu Hui has also decided to include prescription herbal supplements into his diet, to counter the negative side effects the constant ingestion of steroids will have on his liver and kidneys.

"There was a time when I thought I was going to lose him. He had non-

stop seizures for close to 26 hours, even after administering the diazepiam jabs. It's getting harder and harder to make the seizures stop, so we have switched him to steroids. It's such a tough choice to make. I have mixed feelings about feeding him so much steroids. It helps control his seizures but it could potentially shorten his life span drastically. Pluto is only a two-year-old baby, so this is very hard to accept.'

Adopting Pluto has resulted in Shu Hui having to make many adjustments in her life. His attacks come without any warning signs, and she has to constantly be alert and on her toes. She also has to ensure she has enough leave for emergencies. That means no unnecessary holidays.

"My main source of support is actually my father. Pluto adores my father and vice-versa. My dad is a retiree and I was glad he fell in love with Pluto at first sight, so I just let their relationship blossom. I just lost my mother the previous year to cancer so Pluto filled that empty void for my father. Dog and human rely alot on each other.

Not all dog owners can and will commit to caring for an ill dog. Everyone expects their dogs to be healthy and hunky dory but dogs are living creatures too, just like humans. They can, and will, fall ill too. Giving up a dog because of health or age issues is akin to throwing out a sick child or an aged parent and just reflects on how much empathy that person possesses. Even more disgusting are those who heartlessly abandon them on the street, left to their own devices in a cruel, uncaring world. There are always solutions, if you search hard enough. I've also learnt that the Singapore doggie community is a tight knit one with a big heart who will always lend a hand to those who need it.

"Despite his condition, I loved him from the moment I picked him up. He is similar to an autistic child in the way he behaves. I have accepted the fact that he isn't a normal dog but it makes me love him even more.

Apart from his illness, he is actually a very simple dog! He wants to be hugged, touched and loved every day. He spends his mornings basking in the sun next to my dad. He spends the rest of the day following my dad around the house. His favourite sleeping position is right on his chest!

Pluto is super loved and gets (mostly) everything he wants. He loves life but he cannot really enjoy it too much. There are so many things he cannot do.

I used to think it will be nice for him to visit dog cafes and meet friends, run along the beach, enjoy the fresh sea breeze and touch the wet sand. But he can't go

out because he will get excited and his seizures will start. So we don't bring him out. I'd rather keep him safe and happy at home. As a simple canine, all he wants a safe, warm and loving environment.

We have to be strong. Imagine having to inject him with medication every single day. We had to learn how to administer these injections and also pacify him when he whines and cries because of the pain.

Pluto's blindness is getting worse as a result of his illness, yet he has never let his disabilities get in his way. He is still the sweetest dog ever. He will stick his face against our legs lovingly and follow us everywhere

His prognosis is about twelve months. I am totally not prepared for him to leave so soon. One year is really too short for a two-year-old, especially one who had a bad start in life. We may not have much time left with him, but we can make sure he has the best life. And we will never give up on him, no matter what.

When his time is up, I only wish that it is not painful. No screams, no wails. If his time is up, I hope this poor innocent baby will pass on peacefully in his sleep, without the seizures. Yes, I will feel broken but I will keep him forever in my heart."

#DoYouReally WantToHurtMe

It was a Christmas Pearly Looi would never forget for the rest of her life.

She woke up on 26 December 2015 to an ominous email, which read:

"I adopted a male Pomeranian at your adoption drive on 11 July 2015.

I brought the boy to the vet and he was diagnosed with mandibular fracture and severe dental disease. He also has a bad yeast infection on his skin. The doctor vaccinated him and gave him some medication to treat the skin disease. He also advised on the possibility of treatment for his fractured jaw. The surgery would amount to more than $5k. The doctor also advised that surgery may not be advisable as he is a very old dog.

The boy has also infected my existing pom with the serious skin disease and I had to treat the both of them.

A few months have passed and the boy was not able to get along with my other Pomeranian. He was also not able to be toilet trained and would poo and pee all around the house. I have to wake up extra early every day to clear his mess and do the same thing when I am back from work... this has put tremendous stress on me mentally.

Two weeks back, I noticed that he had difficulty walking. I was worried that he may have a fractured leg as he likes to run and jump around. I arranged SANTA *an emergency visit to the vet and was relieved that he does not have any injuries to his leg. However, doctor say that he may be suffering from nerve diseases and in order to diagnose the problem, a CT scan and MRI may be required. The bill again may cost up to $5k. Meanwhile doctor prescribed some anti inflammation medications and advised to monitor the boy.*

The boy is now not as active as before and the problem of soiling around the house has gotten worse.

I am very stressed due to his condition as well as the ability to keep and maintain him. I do not want to cage him or lock him up, as it defeats the purpose of me adopting him in the first place.

Due to a change in jobs, I may be financially tight in the near future. Therefore, I cannot afford more medical treatment for him.

With a heavy heart, I will have to release him back to you for him to be sheltered by someone more capable of taking better care for him."

Santa is a handsome and sociable boy, with the brightest smile, a constantly wagging tail, the softest, most beautiful coat of white fur and a wicked sparkle in his gorgeous eyes. He also had impeccable manners and the most adorable way of asking for treats. There is absolutely no sign that this dog was abused. He's so happy and healthy. Santa is a great example of just how resilient and forgiving dogs really are.

Pearly was a volunteer with the shelter then, and remembered the dog well. She read the email over and over again with a heavy heart, called the owner immediately to better understand Haki the pom's condition and to request for a few days to find a fosterer. It was the festive season and many people were travelling over the Christmas holidays. There was hardly any joy in the Looi household, though. She kept thinking about the poor dog the entire day, and woke up the next morning with a nagging feeling that she had to get Haki out of the house as soon as possible. She requested for the dog immediately.

"When Haki was handed over, he was in a dirty carrier. I opened the carrier, saw a sad looking dog and I knew he was in a very bad condition. His eyes were dull and lifeless. I carried him out and Haki did not move or struggle, which was rather strange. I could see the condition of his front left paw and it didn't appear normal. At this point, I was very upset and angry but decided not to waste any time reproaching his owner or demand any explanations. The only thing on my mind was to get Haki away from him and to my house.

When we got home, the first thing I did was to check Haki thoroughly. My heart sank when I put him on a table and he did not even attempt to stand up. He was extremely unkempt, his nails were very long, ears were filthy and his skin was in a really bad condition. After I trimmed his nails and cleaned his ears, I put him on the floor and he tried to walk but was unable to even stand properly. It was heartbreaking to see this as I remember him to be a physically normal dog before he was adopted."

Pearly named him Santa, which was apt because it was Christmas, but it also meant calmness and peace in the Pali language. He started responding to that name almost immediately, which made his new owner question how much attention he was given in his previous home.

An X-ray revealed a dislocated and fractured right hind leg and suspected neuro damage, which was the cause of his weakness and a bent left paw.

SANTA WHEN FIRST RESCUED

SANTA AFTER HIS SEIZURE,
HIS SCREAMS WERE TERRIFYING

SANTA'S FIRST WEEK

Santa was a retired breeding dog under the care of the shelter before he was rehomed in July 2015 to a guy in his late twenties who stayed alone. Pearly remembers him as quiet, shy and subdued, the only boy in a bunch of rescued poms. Apart from poor dental and a mild skin condition, he was generally healthy and in good shape when he was taken home by his first adopter.

To see him after five months in such a pathetic state really broke everyone's hearts. They suspected that his injuries were as a result of beatings, solely based on everyone's experience dealing with injured dogs. He was probably scruffed on his neck and walloped hard on his bum (perhaps during the failed attempt at toilet training?). It was certainly hard enough to cause the dislocation and fracture.

"I cried like shit on 27 December 2015."

The first two weeks were extremely challenging for Pearly. Santa would go into periodic fits due to hypoglycemia – he would suddenly scream and his whole body would go into a tremor. He was unable to move. He couldn't get up to drink or eat on his own. During the first five days, she did not leave the house for long periods of time as she needed to feed the dog every two hours.

"I could see him gradually regaining energy and life despite his fits and I gradually increased the duration between feeds.

She brought him to two different vets, for peace of mind and a second opinion. It was established that he has a fractured and dislocated right hind leg and a bent left paw, probably due to the injury to the nerves in his neck. He was also anemic, hypoglycemic and very severely dehydrated. They advised against the operation to reattach Santa's dislocated leg as there was a fracture which may cause complications. At that point in time, coupled with his anemia and hypoglycemia, the risks of the surgery were too high.

> **"**
>
> IMO, the most important quality a dog owner should have is to always stand by your dog and never give up on them regardless of circumstances. Even if the outlook appears bleak, stick by the dog till he/she takes the last breath.
>
> The only expectations I have of my dogs are that they are happy during their lifetime and, when the time comes, to have a smooth departure. Everything else is secondary and are non-issues for me.
>
> **"**
>
> PEARLY LOOI

Miraculously, his eyes brightened by the third day. He regained his balance (somewhat) and started to walk (albeit rather awkwardly) for short distances. Even the vet was amazed, and speculated that the leg may have somehow found its way back into the socket, with the scarring tissue helping to reattach the dislocated bone. Amazingly, Santa eventually regained the ability to walk, jump and run without operation or physiotherapy.

"The day Santa showed me he could prance again was when I got back from Panda's (a dog I fostered but loved as my own) cremation. Panda passed away a month after I rescued Santa and the two dogs loved each other. I believe it was Panda blessing him."

With that out of the way, Pearly could get down to treating his skin disease, which turned out to be scabies, a condition that was easily treatable. Again, the suspicions that his previous owner did not bring the dog to the vet began to surface.

"All my friends came over often to visit Santa, and all their dogs rallied around him. He welcomed the company. He was an extremely friendly dog, so I had no idea why the adopter complained that he had social issues. One of the dogs in the pack, Happy, took it upon herself to look after Santa and became his protector.

It is so amazing how much compassion and empathy dogs have compared to some humans."

Pearly also realized that Santa was toilet trained and would always do his business on the pee pads. Santa has never once discharged his waste in any other part of the house since he was rescued by Pearly, so it was really quite amazing the lengths people would go to and the untruths they would fabricate just to give up their dogs.

"Santa is extremely close to me cos probably to him, I was the light of hope when he was despondent. In his initial weeks with me, I would hold his paw whenever he was sleeping and till today, he uses his paw to communicate with me. He still "asks" that I hold his paw when he sleeps at times. He has become a very charming happy boy and much loved by anyone who meets him.

Truth be told, I wasn't sure if he would be able to walk again or survive back then. When I look at him now, it's hard for me to believe he was the same poorly dog whom I saw in Dec 2015."

Looking at the boy, curled up on my lap fast asleep after the excitement of his party, I struggled to understand how anyone could ever lay a land on something so gentle and trusting. I have never met his ex-owner, and I have no desire to ever want to ever cross paths with such a specimen.

Santa is truly a miracle boy, saved from a life of abuse from an irresponsible, deceitful, cruel man who threw him out, and was healed through lots of genuine love and TLC.

"I have learnt many life lessons from my dogs. No matter how adverse the circumstances may seem, never ever give up.

Every life is precious.

Unconditional love creates miracles."

#SavingAll MyLoveForYou

Snuffles was a nine-year-old Shih Tzu adopted by Carolyn several years ago. He was blind and deaf and suffered from an enlarged heart. She lost him to congestive heart failure in October 2017.

Carol and I were both on the same page with regards to our views on adoption, so, unbeknownst to her, I kept a lookout for another suitable dog amongst the many rescues in the shelter I volunteered at. I knew it was a matter of time before the right dog came along.

There was one particular dog that I felt would be especially right for Carol. She was a lovely little girl, pleasantly plump with the more gorgeously soulful eyes. Some of the shelter volunteers called her Bloated. Another called her Fatty! I re-christianed her Manja, because she had just so much love to give despite all that she had gone through.

I invited Carol to an adoption drive in October to meet Manja, with no strings attached. It was simply just for her to 'look see'.

"I had attended a few adoption drives but none of the dogs had really connected with me. As I went to this, I had a sneaky suspicion that this would be the one time I would walk away with a new pup, but I still tried to be nonchalant and non-committal.

When we got there, Daniel said he would go into the enclosure to look for her, but got distracted by another volunteer. While waiting for him, so many scruffy (it had rained earlier) lovely dogs came up to me. Among them, I saw a sweet yearning face peering up at me beseechingly, her little tail going a mile a minute. As we were not allowed to touch the dogs, I spoke softly to this darling little pup for several minutes. She finally wandered off but I watched her for a while. She was a little timid, very wary of being underfoot yet following closely and wagging her tail at one of the volunteers. I didn't see her going up to any other visitors. When Daniel came back and identified her as the dog he wanted to introduce me to, I knew that was it. They say the dog chooses you, and until then I didn't know what it meant."

But first, there were the formalities of pre-screening and an administrative briefing. When Carol made that decision, I got her an adoption form and a queue number.

GRACIE

"When my turn came, a shelter volunteer asked about my background – did I had a pet before, what happened to it etc. She then briefed me on the special nature of rescued ex-breeder dogs – she would pee and poo anywhere because she didn't know better, she may never be 100% pee pad trained et al. She would be fearful of the collar and leash and would need patience to learn to walk with one. She could be timid and may take time to warm up to human contact. There could be inherent health issues as with all breeder dogs, and she could have required more medical care.

> **"**
> Why did I choose to adopt my dog?
> There are so many dogs out there who need a home, and I don't trust the breeders' ethics. If we don't create a demand, they will not feel driven to create puppy mills. And rescue dogs appreciate the blessings you give them, are completely loving and provide you with such joy.
> **"**

CAROLYN NG

DAY OF ADOPTION

I had to promise to take her to the vet within a week, sterilise her as soon as possible and register her with AVA. A volunteer would be assigned to follow-up with me and possibly make a home visit."

After signing the papers and making a small payment to cover the cost of vaccinations, food and care at the shelter, Carol left Manja with the shelter for one final night whilst she set about making the necessary arrangements to prepare the house for her arrival.

"When I went to pick her up the next day, the volunteers were amazingly bathing and grooming all the pups for that day's adoption drive and she got a pretty trim too! I decided to call her Gracie because of her sweet nature.

A friend helped drive us home, and I carried her in my arms throughout the entire journey. She was quiet, but perked up when I put her down, so I realised that she was a little afraid of being carried at a height. When we exited the car, I walked her downstairs for a bit and she fought the collar and leash. After she had the chance to pee, I carried her up and finally put her down when we entered the apartment."

Gracie knew at once she was home. She bravely sniffed every corner of the apartment, and followed her new mama everywhere. She even tolerated her first shower in her new home. Carol won her over with ear scratches, which she loved.

FIRST DAY AT HOME

Gracie peed all over the apartment that day, watched her new mama go about her activities and continued exploring the flat. They slept together on the cold hard floor that night. Gracie did not know what to make of the soft bed nor the pee pads, having never seen them in her life. But she settled in immediately.

"It was challenge leaving her the next day for work so I kept her in the kitchen with her water bowl and pee pad. I came home to find pee on both the pee pad and the floor. I praised her when she got it right and would scold her gently if she made a mess. She would look repentant and I could tell she was trying.

We visited the vet and discovered she had slight tick fever, scabies and a bacterial ear infection, but thankfully nothing worse. She was shaven down at the groomers so that we could allow her skin to heal better – she looked really sheepish and rat-like for a while!

She got used to walking with a harness, loved her morning and evening walks and took a couple of weeks to figure out that she was supposed to pee on her walks. She would initially only pee on hard floors (having not much experience with grass in her puppy mill prison), and balked at walking in the field. Within a month she was peeing on grass but would still poo on hard ground.

She resisted sleeping in the doggy bed for three weeks until I did a petting session on it one day. She has loved it since and will switch between the bed and floor to sleep.

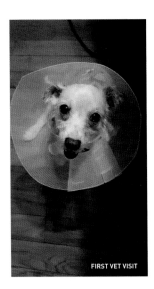

FIRST VET VISIT

When she went into heat, I freaked out because at first I thought she had UTI. My previous dog was a boy so it was a learning journey for me. She wore a diaper for a week, and quickly got used to it."

Three months into her adoption, Gracie became more courageous on her walks and even leads the way sometimes. She doesn't fight the harness and is not so easily startled by vehicles, unfamiliar structures and loud sounds. She is still wary of the chew toy but mummy and daughter have fun playing peekaboo with a towel. She loves building a nest with a towel on her bed, loves her snacks, and her favourite activity is exposing her belly for lots of loving belly rubs.

She is 80% pee pad trained but still has occasional accidents around the house. Carol accepts it as part and parcel of their journey together. Helping a new dog assimilate into a new environment requires plenty of patience, and Carol has oodles of it.

"I need to teach her how to adapt to our world and understand our habits and our rules. It is also about knowing and understanding each other. I am firm with her, but praise her and pet her when she does something well. She learns fast, and I try to use simpler words to help her understand things around her.

You need to be able to spend time to understand your dog's needs, why they behave the way they do, try different methods to help them learn, and always show them love. Be firm yet loving, never abusive, be open to the dog's personality whatever they may be, accept that there are some things you can't change, and be open to new adventures together."

Six months down the road, Gracie has still not gotten the health all-clear from her vet. She is still in and out

of the clinic for X-rays and consultations. Throughout this entire process, Gracie's happy demeanour and calm temperament has helped give strength to Carol. Her unconditional love has made all the challenges thrown in their path a bit more bearable. And, along the way, Carol has also discovered the joys of discussing dog poo and their health implications!

"Gracie has a great spirit and is such a gentle loving soul. My main priority is to keep her safe and for her to be happy and healthy.

I am so proud of how far she has come, and how she has become more content. She loves me unconditionally and because of that, I am trying to find ways to give her a stable, balanced and loving household."

#TakeA ChanceOnMe

"We spent about 30 minutes at the adoption drive, mostly looking at the female dogs, and were about to leave when we decided to walk past the boy's pen. Then I spotted Rufus, sitting by himself in the middle of the field. The other dogs were running around him. There was just something about him sitting there by himself that drew me to him.

When Terence went to the fence to take a closer look, Rufus came over to meet him. And paw touched finger. When that happened, we knew we had a new member of the family."

Rufus is a cute little French bulldog that Wee Teck and his partner Terence adopted recently. It was an unplanned visit to a random adoption drive that changed their lives forever.

"About a year ago, we went to an adoption drive, and nearly adopted then. On 20 August 2018, Terence and I decided on impulse to visit the drive again. He had just moved into his new home and there was a ton of stuff to do, but we decided to drop everything and just go take a look.

We sauntered around aimlessly, not sure if we were ready to adopt after the deaths of our last two dogs. Phoebe and Lazy were both 15-and-a-half when they passed on, six months apart. Their deaths affected me tremendously, especially Lazy's, as he had been with me since he was a puppy. I became impossible to be with.

Emotionally, I couldn't do it. Then we met Rufus.

But first, there was the screening process. It was nerve-racking because of the number of questions asked. I was a little put off, but I understood why it had to be done. Better the bitter truth and reality about adopting a former breeding dog now than to get a nasty insummountable shock when things happen. I filled up a few forms in a daze, and then, Rufus was ours.

We soon found ourselves in an Uber with him in our arms. That was when we realised how much he sheds. We RUFUS *were covered with his hair by the end of the trip. We also realised he farts a lot. But we were too busy running through a list of things we needed to get for him to be bothered by his flatulence.*

When we brought him home and carried him through the door, he looked tentative and scared. I guess it was a big deal for him too, and he had probably never seen a house before.

We knew so little about his former life, other than he was a breeding dog rescued a month before we adopted him. But there was no time to ponder. We were completely unprepared for him as we were literally in the middle of moving when we adopted him! We brought him to the groomer for a shower, and ran around in a mad rush to purchase everything we needed whilst he was there.

We did not have anything prepared. Our own bed had not arrived, and most of the furniture was still shrink wrapped. We dug out some old tee shirts and made a makeshift bed for him. We tied another tee-shirt into a knot and turned it into a toy for him. His groomer gave him a bag of food and his first leash. At the end of the evening, our new house had a new dog!"

Rufus spent most of his first month with Terence, who was on leave then. He was very quiet the first few days, and they both wondered if he could bark. He would follow Terence around the house occasionally, or sleep in his bed. He was not fussy with his food and ate everything that was given to him.

Toilet training was a challenge. The boys had forgotten how much patience is needed for that. As he had spent all his years in a tiny cage, they felt guilty confining him to an area in the kitchen, but eventually, after many puddles of pee and mountains of poo, they had to.

"The guilt multiplied when we had to keep him there during the day, when we were at work. But we realised that toilet training was more for our sanity than anything else, so we decided to be patient with him and let him learn slowly.

Walking him was a huge task. He would take two steps, pause for 15 minutes before taking another two. It took us all of six months and the help of a trainer before he felt confident enough to walk with the leash, and whilst it is much better now, there are still times when he has his moments. We have learnt to let him take his time. After all, the walks are for him, not us, so we let him sniff to his hearts content.

❝

There will be challenges when you adopt, especially when it has been through so much so there must be patience. It breaks my heart to see a family adopt a dog, then return the dog just cos the challenges got overwhelming. There isn't a 'at least he was in a home for a while' logic because it is just cruel. So adopt only when you are absolutely ready - emotionally, financially and physically.

❞

YEOH WEE TECK & TERENCE TAN

We brought him to the vet, who gave us a list of things we needed to do for him, so that has become his routine. He was advised to put on weight, and he has done so in a big way! Thankfully, he is healthy(ish). The challenge is keeping ME in check. Each scab, each mark drives me into a frenzy!

There were so many moments during the first month when we thought 'why are we doing this again?' There were times when I thought of the heartache I felt when we lost our two kids. But every night, I would look at him sleeping at the foot of the bed and know that we did the right thing.

My family consider Rufus the family dog now and fawn over him constantly. To me, he is my sleep mate, and I have gotten used to his snoring. Before he came into our lives, we could go on vacations or parties or gym without any consideration. Things are now planned with him in mind. But I don't mind it one single bit.

A few days into his stay at Bedok, Terence sent me a picture of Rufus on his hind legs, staring at the TV. He had never seen one before and did not know what to make of it. That made me tear. Of course he soon got sick of it and ignores it today.

Rufus has moved on since his days siring puppies for sale. Or so we thought. One day, at the pool, whilst waiting for our turn to swim, we caught Rufus trying to hump every single female dog there. I guess he thought he was still at work, and old habits die hard!

I think it was fate that brought us all together, that made us drop everything in the middle of frantic house moving to visit the adoption drive. When we got our first two dogs, we did not know better and purchased them from pet shops. Over the years, we have read and researched about mills and what the dogs go through, so we now know better. When it was time, adoption was the only option for us.

Rufus loves being with people. For a dog that went through so much, no thanks to greedy humans, he is forgiving. That is the best way to live – to just let the past go and move forward. Enjoy the treats and the belly rubs now

I'm so glad we took a chance on him... and him with us."

#MyHappyPill

"I was contacted by a rescuer named Hilda. She had a Chow Chow puppy on her hands that she needed help with. She was about five months old, still in need of mummy's milk and love, but her breeding dog mother was torn away from her as she had been adopted and was due to be sent overseas to her new home.

She reached out to me because of my knowledge of the breed.

I absolutely do not support irresponsible breeding nor buying from them, either directly or indirectly (through pet shops), and was afraid the breeder might replace the mother in the mill with this puppy. She would be ready to breed in a month, so I knew I had to act fast to prevent this from happening.

I headed to the groomer, where they had placed this dog, and I secretly know that she would probably be exploited as a breeding dog should she fall into the wrong hands. My instincts kicked in and I decided to bring her home."

Eos was a very bony pup at the time of her rescue. She was suffering from malnutrition and her fur was badly tangled. The groomer allowed Plex to hold her and they bonded instantly. She could tell from the young pup's eyes that she was calling out for help and decided to give her a proper home to live her life.

"Everything happened in an overwhelming rush. She sat quietly in my car and rested the entire trip. I took this as a sign that she felt safe with me. When we got home, I introduced her to the other dogs in the family. They sniffed her and she responded by climbing over them in excitement. I did my best to put all the dogs at ease with proper introductions, and there was acceptance all round."

EOS

159

66

To err is human - to forgive, canine.

99

PLEX CHEN

Plex's most important concern was medical. It was obvious that she did not get enough nutrition at the puppy mill. She probably didn't have access to much food then, for she would dash to the bowl and gobble down the food in the rush. Her new pawrent did some research and found out that most puppy mills do not cater to individual nutritional needs of the dogs. The food was put into a huge tub and it was every dog for him or herself. The smaller and weaker dogs usually got shoved out of the way and would be too weak to fight for their share of the food. Eos was so under-weight and small for her age and this was something Plex had to address immediately.

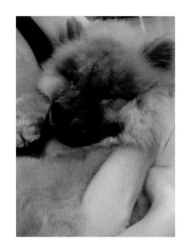

Potty and leash training were next. Plex had the help of her other Chow Chow, Jetta to guide her.

"It took me less than three days for me to achieve success, thanks to my very efficient sidekick."

Eos freaks out when she sees any male figures approaching. She would start to back off and growl, and sometimes even snap if the guy attempts to touch her. Her new family suspected that she had been abused by men at the mill, and worked hard to address this fear.

I engaged the services of an animal communicator despite my skepticism in an attempt to delve into Eos' past. I was shocked by what she told me. For the longest time, I would wake in the middle of the night feeling extremely nauseous and weak in the legs. I would try to induce vomit to make me feel better. I consulted doctors but was told each time that it is stress related. Eos told the animal communicator all about my problem, which she code-named 'Cold Spot' and suggested a course of action should it happen again. Some months later, I went for a massage and the masseuse told me the exact same thing as Eos. She even referenced the exact same pressure points that Eos had mentioned! It changed my opinion of animal communicators completely.

I have had fourteen dogs throughout my life. Most of them were given up by friends of my parents because they did not have the commitment or loved them enough to keep them. Some of them were posted overseas and did not want to bring their dogs with them. Others were abandoned because their kids had lost interest in them. It made me realise how irresponsible and self-centered some dog owners can be. I shut my ears to these lame excuses and concentrated on helping the animals.

I now have four dogs under my care at home. I worry that I will be biased in giving one more love than the others and am careful to strike a balance with them. Ever since adopting Eos, I now have more responsibilities, which I am happy to shoulder. She is a simple dog with simple needs. She gets along so well with my older dog and takes the cue from him.

Eos is indeed my happy pill."

#ARainbow InTheDark

When humans are in conflict with each other, their pets are often collateral damage. People who use their pets as pawns are aplenty. Thankfully, there are also angels amongst us who step in to save the day. Dogs have that innate sixth sense to identify these angels, and recognize that turning point in their lives.

Here is the amazing story of two goldies who found their savior in their darkest hours.

Leia is best buds with Cesar and Chelsea, whom she stays with occasionally when her papa's work keeps him away from home. The two dogs reside as king and queen, and Leia enjoys her playtime with them. Cesar and Chelsea are the most adorable dogs who love nothing more than to flop next to you, head on thigh, waiting for massages and belly rubs.

Their happy and healthy demeanour belies their sad origin stories, which, thankfully, came with silver linings for each of them. For, emerging from the dark clouds surrounding their respective ex-owner's palavas came their lovely angel.

"When I moved to a landed home in 2010, I decided it was time to get another dog. Volunteer stints with the SPCA and other dog shelters in my younger days steered me towards adopting instead of purchasing from a pet shop. I searched the net endlessly for a dog that would be a good fit. I visited many adoption drives and went through many homestay trials. There were many dogs I liked but we did not have that special affinity. I had a particular affinity for Golden Retrievers and kept a lookout for them. I chanced upon a picture of a sweet goldie peeking from under a table and my heart skipped a beat. I contacted the owner immediately and arranged a viewing. There were several enquiries already but I cajoled them into giving me an appointment.

I got terribly lost in the maze of flats in Woodlands on the day I was supposed to meet him. I got a call from the owner asking if I was still interested and I  *screamed 'Yes!' down the phone. I was so anxious and afraid I would loose him to someone else. After driving around for an hour, I finally located the block and ran towards the meeting place in the void deck. I saw a guy holding on to a golden boy in the distance. When I was about 15 metres away, he dropped the leash and the dog sprinted towards me with a funny bunny hop. After that initial greeting, he circled me, sniffed till he was satisfied and sat down by my side, as if to claim me. Something just connected between the two of us at that moment. He chose me. It was a special sign.*

I found out he had severe hip dysplasia, which accounted for his funny gait, but it did not deter me. I was ready to take on the challenge and asked for a trial visit.

Cookie's owners brought him over on a Sunday afternoon. I was told that Cookie was an extremely picky eater, so I cooked some chicken and potatoes as a welcome snack. Cookie was quite calm when he entered the house and proceeded to check out the surroundings. He walked around the front porch and the garden to the side garden and the backyard. He christened his visit with a pee and a poo. I saw that as a sign that he was marking his turf as his home, and praised him profusely. My husband John took an instant liking to his calmness and obedience. Cookie chomped down the chicken and potatoes and settled comfortably on the front porch as the humans began the discussion to sort out his adoption.

The owners were initially not confident that we could accord Cookie the love and care but we managed to convince them of our suitability and sincerity after a lengthy discussion. Cookie was officially adopted on the 26th August 2011, just two weeks shy of his first birthday. It was a very exciting day as I prepared for his arrival. He arrived with his soon-to-be-ex-owners in the late evening, and we allowed them to spend time alone with the dog before leaving. I took Cookie for a walk soon after, so that the owners could take their leave. I did not want the dog to see his owners driving away, in case he felt abandoned.

We re-named him Cesar and promised him a better life.

I consulted a couple of specialist vets on his hip issue and started a search for his medical history. I called the clinic he visited as a puppy and gathered as much information as I could. I decided to put off surgery till he absolutely needed it and opted instead for a rehabilitation programme of therapeutic and targeted exercises, nutrition and supplements.

Cesar was still very much a puppy, with extreme puppy behaviour when we adopted him at 11 months. I engaged a one-on-one trainer for Cesar three days after he was adopted. We worked together on Cesar's obedience and discipline as well as the rehab of Cesar's hips. Cesar was easy to train and very obedient.

In the course of training and disciplining Cesar, we suspected that he could have been beaten or slapped before. He was very scared and retreated when we raised our hands towards him, even if it was just to pat him on the head. We helped him get over that through positive actions and words and lots of patience.

One of the conditions of the adoption was to allow a visit from his ex-owners three months later. The owners had initially requested for more periodic visits but I advised against it, as it may confuse the dog.

The meeting was arranged at a neutral place. We decided on Bishan dog run. When his ex-owners entered the enclosure, Cesar ran to greet them in the same manner he does with all humans. His ex-mom was emotional but Cesar ran off to play after the initial greeting. The difference in the new Cesar was very clear and they knew it. He was more confident and his hind legs were stronger. I observed Cesar closely for any reactions but he was oblivious to his former pawrents. From that moment, I knew that Cesar was totally ours.

After spending half an hour in the enclosure observing Cesar as he played with his doggie friends, they left, accompanied by my husband. I stayed with Cesar. They never requested to visit again.

Cesar was not a healthy pup, growing up, the result of irresponsible breeding by a puppy mill in the eastern part of the island. He was always ill and had symptoms of parvo-virus. He was hospitalized and they almost lost him. But Nurse AJ never gave up on him. She carried the puppy whenever she could, encouraged him to fight on and nursed him back to health. Four years after we adopted Cesar, we bumped into AJ at a community pet event. She was overjoyed to reconnect with the dog and shared all the stories of his early days with us.

[L-R]
CHELSEA, CESAR

Cesar today is well and healthy as can be. He will be nine soon, but shows no sign of slowing down. Because of Cesar, I delved into learning all I can about canine nutrition, health, targeted supplementing and dog wellness. I became more health conscious and transformed my own life so that I can enjoy more of life with him. We went on short and long walks. During the first three years of Cesar's rehab, John and I made time to bring him swimming almost every weekend. I hate the sun but for Cesar, I braved it all. I said goodbye to my moon-kissed fair skin forever.

From a very nervous and fearful puppy who could not even cross a small drain, Cesar has grown into a calm and confident dog. Papa would patiently coax and show him the way to leap across drains. Cesar used to be afraid even of a stationary motorbike. Through patience and exposure, we slowly built his trust. Through building up his health and muscles, Cesar became more confident in his movements.

Lots of my precious lunch breaks were given up just so I could rush home to keep him company especially if a thunderstorm was brewing. Cesar is afraid of thunder. I built a cosy corner in the house for him to hide in, but I always tried to be around whenever there is an impending storm.

No matter how late I work, I will always make time for our special bonding night walk and car rides. My hubs always says that our dog leads a better life than us – he eats better and gets more attention than the humans!

Since I left corporate employment to start my own franchisee business, Cesar has become my ambassador and partner. I take him on some of my appointments and he enjoys the car rides tremendously. I cherish our time together. Our bond has grown even stronger during the last four years of our special partnership. One year, when we were planning for Cesar's birthday party, we heard that his ex-mom was in town and invited her. There were lots of changes in her life and she was no longer living in Singapore. She saw how happy and healthy her former dog had become, and the love we had for each other, and left feeling emotional. Cesar treated her like a stranger, and we could see how she wished he was still her Cookie.

With all the checks in place and all that emotion from the ex-owners, why then was Cesar given up? It stemmed from a soured relationship. Mr A had bought the dog for his girlfriend, Ms K, but her mother never took to him. Mummy had her own dog and favoured that, ignoring Cookie. He grew up a sickly, nervous and under-socialised puppy. His genetic hip dysplasia was diagonised at seven months. When the couple broke up, the girl and her family decided they did not want to keep Cookie, and neither did the guy. They decided to rehome him.

Their loss is my big gain!"

When Cesar turned six, Lisa and John discussed the possibility of adopting another dog. As she was a volunteer with several dog shelters and rescue associations, and was active with helping to foster and rehome them, she saw many potential dogs, but none of them "made my heart flutter the way Cesar did many years ago."

On 1 April 2017, I got a call from a friend who heads the pedigree rehoming department of a dog rescue shelter. A female Golden Retriever was being surrendered to the shelter on April Fools Day!. He asked if I could help foster, rehome or adopt her, so I brought Cesar along.

We met this beautiful girl at her home, a beautiful apartment in the Holland district. There was an air of chill when we walked in and it wasn't from the cold. Her owners were going through a separation as well as a relocation to another country, and she did not factor in either one of their plans.

CESAR WITH NURSE AJ

CHELSEA'S FIRST DAY IN HER FOREVER HOME

Ria the goldie was a happy, carefree girl with a beautiful top coat of long fur. On closer examination, her back and belly were covered with hotspots and rash from a skin allergy. I was immediately taken by her but I had to get Cesar's approval.

It was important that Cesar accept Ria. My worries were unnecessary. The initial introduction went smoothly and the two dogs settled comfortably with each other. According to Ria's papa, she is extremely selective with the dogs she allows into her space. When I saw how comfortable both dogs were with each other, I agreed on a home trial.

I was handed a cardboard box which contained Ria's belongings – some leftover kibbles, old toys, medicated shampoo, an odd harness and other little necessities. It was almost like 'good bye, good riddance'. Ria's mama then came out from her room briefly to say hello and disappeared almost immediately. There were no goodbye hugs or any sign of love for Ria. I felt very sad. Ria was being given up like a piece of old junk, but I knew that she deserved better than this cold, unloving home.

We gathered the stuff and brought Ria and Cesar for a short walk. I was handed Ria's vet records and told that she was sterilised and had a long history of hotspots and skin issues. Her papa tried to self-medicate with a dose or two of vitamin C, which obviously did not work. Ria was fed a diet of kibbles. Apart from a morning and an evening walk with papa, she was left by her lonesome self for most part of the day. Papa said goodbye to her and promised to visit after she was settled. Mama watched. I never heard from either of them after that day.

Five days later, I signed the papers, formally adopting Ria. I celebrated her fresh start by renaming her Chelsea.

Chelsea settled into our home very quickly without too much fuss. I found out that she was administered several doses of steroids and antibiotics in the past. Her immunity was extremely low. She seemed to be allergic to many food items and had behavioural and anxiety issues. She would chew on her paws and bite herself, which resulted in the frequent hotspots. We carried out food allergy tests on her so that we could determine what she could and could not eat. The kibbles she had been fed were totally disagreeable with her, so we switched her to home cooked food and placed her on a strict diet.

Her rehab journey was fraught with much stress as we decided to steer clear of unnecessary medications. Chelsea broke out frequently in hotspots, suffered from yeast infection and had constant ear problems. We had to wipe her down her several times daily to get rid of the yeast, disinfect her hotspots and clean her ears, all of which she allowed us to do, and endured patiently. There were many frustrating moments. Just when we thought she is cleared, another wave of attack comes around. Thankfully I perservered.

Despite her health setbacks, Chelsea is a feisty, fun-loving, carefree gal. She runs around like a bull in a china shop; she swims like a dolphin and plays with gay abandon. She has bonded very well with Cesar and always knows her boundaries with her elder brother. Through Chelsea, Cesar got his groove back. The two dogs wrestle daily. Walks are not complete without each other.

Chelsea's health and immunity has improved greatly. She still gets the occasional hotspot but they heal very quickly. Her yeasty discoloured skin has cleared and fur has sprouted on the previously baldy infected patches.

My two dogs have become so much a part of my life and taught me lots of life lessons. I tear even at the very thought that I will lose them one day. For now I just want them to be in the best of health and for us to enjoy our lives together."

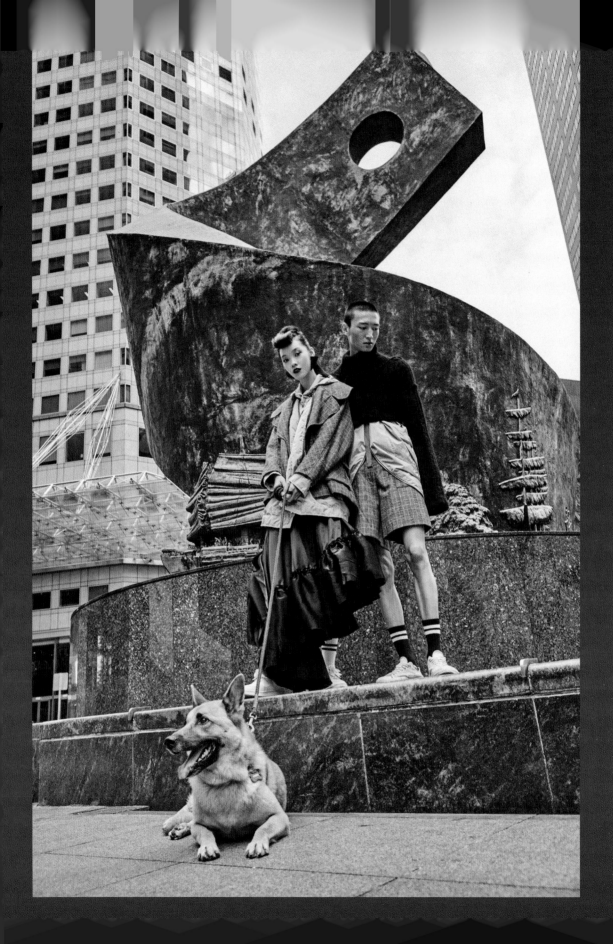

"

The dogs don't judge. They don't care if you have a bad past. They just love you back.

"

TIA TORRES

"

*There are no stupid dogs.
There are lots of people who
haven't learnt to effectively read,
engage with, motivate, set realistic
expectations for, communicate with
and teach their dogs.*

"

ERIN MOORE
PAWSITIVE CONNECTION DOG TRAINING

#BoulevardOf BrokenDreams

I knew (of) Maya long before we actually met. I happened to be scrolling through Facebook one lazy Sunday afternoon when a photograph of male model Derrick Lee popped up and stopped me in my tracks. It was his beautiful lithe companion that had me reaching for my phone to text if he was open to arranging a threesome playdate. *"She's extremely skittish, very shy and not good around people"* was the reply, his disappointment evident in the short text.

I never forgot about Maya, his beautiful Singapore Special, and constantly asked about her. When I adopted Leia, the subject of playdates cropped up again. *"One day, when the kids are ready"*, I remember saying. *"I'm afraid that day may never come"* was Derrick's sad response.

I asked him about his pessimistic answer and his voice filled with emotion.

Maya became part of his family on 17 July 2014. She has brought much joy and happiness to the household and the family constantly remind themselves of how lucky they are to have her in their lives.

Maya, however, wasn't always so lucky. This is her story.

She was found hiding under a car at Sembawang Park by Ben and Adriel. She was about three months old. The boys brought her home to nurse her and to give her a safe sanctuary, and started reaching out to their friends and followers on Twitter for help. Charis was a friend of Ben's, and she found out about the dog.

Co-incidently, Charis is also Derrick's friend.

Back then, Derrick was volunteering weekly at Madam Wong's Shelter as a dog walker. She contacted him to help the boys out, and so, on Sunday 9 February 2014, the four of them took the pup to a vet in nearby Ang Mo Kio to scan for a possible microchip and to also check on her health and general well-being. The nurses asked for her name and Derrick christened her Maya from one of his favourite movies, *Eight Below*.

Maya was healthy but unfortunately, she did not belong to anyone. All of them knew then that they had to find her a home.

They put the word out on social media, and through the power of Instagram and Facebook, they managed to find a fosterer for her that very day. Maya was transported over immediately and handed over, with no screening, paperwork or questions asked.

Derrick paid her a visit on 16 February and found a happy pup. It was then that the fosterer, a young Chinese millennial, informed Derrick that she wanted to adopt Maya.

Alls well that ends well, they thought, and everyone went their own separate ways.

Some time between May and June the same year, Derrick received a call from "Young Chinese Millennial" that her family business was not doing well and that she was no longer capable of caring for Maya. He did not follow up as he was busy.

A few months later, he was scrolling through Facebook when he stumbled upon a picture of a rescued puppy that resembled Maya. She even had the same collar that he had bought for her. Maya, at seven months of age, had been cruelly abandoned and found (yet again!) at Sembawang Park.

When he confronted "Young Chinese Millennial", he realised it wasn't the worst of it.

She had passed the dog to another adopter without his prior knowledge, claiming that her family did not have the finances to take care of the dog any more. She found a random couple and simply handed Maya over without knowing anything about them or if they were capable of being suitable pawrents. She then washed her hands of the matter.

She had absolutely no idea that Maya had been abandoned, but did not seem at all the least interested in that fact. She did not ask after Maya, enquire about her well being or offer to help. Derrick knew then that she really didn't care, and focused his attention on the dog instead.

Maya, meanwhile, had been picked up by a kindly Indian lady, who was a volunteer at ASD, a local AWG (Animal Welfare Group). Derrick contacted her, they met, and through their own CSI, slowly pieced the poor pup's story together.

"Young Chinese Millennial" found the new adopter through a mutual friend, and passed the dog over to them. Maya's new owners, a young Indian couple, played with her for a day, grew sick of her and left her at Sembawang Park the next day. The couple contacted "Kindly Indian Lady" through their aunt who had adopted a dog from ASD, and requested that she come rescue the dog immediately, with the

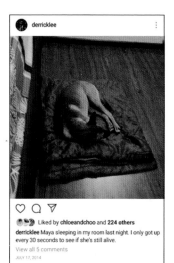

threat that they would call the authorities (and the risk that the pup would be euthanised).

"Kindly Indian Lady" took urgent leave and rushed to pick Maya up. She fostered her for a week, before passing her on to her friend, who took over fostering duties. They were both responsible for posting Maya's story on Facebook, which led to Derrick connecting with the ladies.

When "Kindly Indian Lady" tried to follow up with "Young Indian Couple" for more information, they filed a police report against her for harassment and investigations had to cease.

There wasn't much they could do, so they focused their energies into finding a home for Maya. During this time, Derrick would spend almost every single night with the pup. Days turned into weeks. They brought Maya to every adoption drive they knew of but couldn't get her adopted. She was traumatised and reactive, and why wouldn't she be? At seven months of age, she had already been passed from one home to another with such frequency, and God only knows what other traumas she'd experienced.

When project ADORE, supported by the major Singapore animal welfare groups, became a permanent scheme, Derrick decided to adopt Maya.

On 17 July, he brought her home for the first time.

"My parents were notified prior to Maya coming home. Maya was only supposed to be on a homestay with us for a week, I remembered that first day very vividly. I was trying to get Maya to stay with us permanently. So it was very stressful as I had to make sure she made a good impression. I was so afraid that she might start barking and peeing everywhere.

To my surprise, Maya performed exceedingly well. My parents and I sometimes talk about it and we wondered if she knew that she was being evaluated back then. Within the first week, Maya had bonded very well with my parents. She became especially close to my mother.

I was still worried because even though my parents didn't mention that the seven days were up, they didn't explicitly say that Maya was allowed to continue staying with us. Because of Maya's backstory, the only dog I wanted was her and I wanted to take care of her."

Finally, on his dad's birthday and a week before he enlisted for National Service, Derrick's folks said that they will help take care of Maya and he would have nothing to worry about. On that faithful day in August, Maya officially became the fifth member of the Lee family.

Maya has grown up to be a most beautiful canine. She has certain physical characteristics that resemble a Belgian Malinois. Others (like myself) have mistaken her for a German Shepherd.

She has assimilated very well into family life. Derrick and her sleep together almost every day. *"There was period of time that she stopped coming to my room because I was hardly home. I was always busy with work and school. Since the third quarter of 2018, I have been making a point to go home early to spend more time with her. In 2019, I hope to build an even closer bond with her."*

Five years on, the trauma that Maya faced still lingers. It continues to haunt her till this very day. She still suffers from anxiety and nervousness, and is skittery around people.

"It pains me that Maya went through so much when there was so much that I could have done for her but I just didn't have the time to follow-up. I was always busy but truth of the matter was, I was just busy being lazy and irresponsible.

I regret it today. I regret it everyday.

I owe it to Maya to give her a good time for the rest of her life."

I hold strong to a belief that you should only either adopt or purchase responsibly. By responsible, I mean buying from a reputable breeder and not backyard breeders and puppy shops.

Years back, I did a research study on puppy mills, animal abuse and euthanasia, and I came across a quote which goes like this:

**'When you adopt a shelter pet, you save two lives.
The one you adopt, and the one that takes its place'.**

Since then, I have been an advocate for pet adoption.

DERRICK LEE

#Stop!InThe NameOfLove

"The car came to a screeching halt as we swung to the far side of the road and jammed on the brakes. My friend leapt out, arms flailing like Moses as she parted the sea of vehicles and headed for the pup. She scooped the terrified animal into her arms and ran back to the car, waving the stunned drivers on like a monarch dismissing her subjects, before plopping the dog at my feet and jumping back into the driver's seat"

I sat, listening in rapt wonder as Michelle Teo recounted the tale of how she rescued her dog.

Pasha and Leia were fellow models at the GoodDogPeople doggie runway show, and ended up hanging with each other backstage at the show the entire day. Her calm aura was in absolute stark contrast to the crazy drama of her traffic-stopping rescue.

"We'd gone to Jalan Kayu for a prata breakfast. As we were leaving, we noticed buses swerving crazily and honking madly. And we wondered why. That's when we saw Pasha: a tiny little puppy running madly on the road. We decided we needed to get her off the road, otherwise she wasn't going to stand a chance.

She was running frantically and zig zagging a little. She was clearly terrified and trying to get somewhere. We think she was trying to find her mother and her pack.

There was a lot of honking of horns. I think people were trying to get off the road for her safety. One of the buses almost hit her before swerving dangerously.

We needed to find the right time to stop the car on the side of the road without compromising anyone's safety. And we needed to do it immediately."

Pasha finally made it safely into Michelle's car.

"Her look of relief just broke my heart and she simply flopped down and slept the entire way to SPCA where we thought we should leave her. I think I  *fell in love with Pasha the minute she turned to look at me with her sad eyes and furrowed brow. And she was so trusting – as if she knew already that she'd found her forever home."*

"

Adopting a dog is a huge commitment. Dogs depend on you for everything but in turn they are loyal, loving and unconditional. If you can't make time to potty train your dog, bathe them, walk them everyday, take them to the vet, feed them proper food, and just spend time with them, then don't adopt a dog.

They're hard work but the pay-offs are limitless.

"

MICHELLE TEO

At SPCA, the ladies at reception told Michelle and her companion that there was a chance Pasha might not get adopted as no one knew how big she would grow to. If she didn't find a home, she might end up being put down.

"That just broke my heart and I knew then that we couldn't leave her behind. I cried as I couldn't imagine that puppy not having a home to be safe in. The ladies at SPCA were incredibly kind and they clearly felt so sad seeing her. But I think they sensed that one of us would take the puppy if we knew there was a possibility she might not be re-homed".

So that brown little puppy ended up back in the car.

"The ladies at SPCA suggested we take the puppy to the vet to check her health and to ensure she didn't have any severe issues. They even supplied us with a list of clinics that would be open on a Sunday".

They randomly selected one and took her there. They did not have an appointment so they knew a long wait lay ahead of them.

"Our tiny little girl – she couldn't have been more than a few months and could be held in one hand – fell right asleep while we sat at the clinic, surrounded by designer dogs and sympathetic humans. I knew as we sat there waiting that this dog had found us and was meant to be a part of my life. And it was a little scary as I'd never had a pet in my life and we had no idea how things would turn out. It really was a leap of faith – on both our parts.

The vet we had was incredibly kind and she even gave Pasha a huge hug. She was checked thoroughly and we were asked to come back another day when the blood test results were in as well for her vaccination.

We were also given a great deal of advice about bathing her and monitoring her both on this first (and many subsequent) visits."

The drive home after the vet was all logistics focused: how to register her? What should I call her? What should I feed her? What shampoo to use? What about her bed? What if she peed in the house? What about the collar? Leash? Food?

They did some quick shopping before getting her back to Michelle's home. She was given a bath. Michelle had to figure out where to put her for the night. The kitchen became her little play space, so she put up a makeshift gate to contain the young pup.

The dog barked the ENTIRE night and MIchelle ended up having to stay with her in the kitchen the whole time. She barked all the next day as well and her new owner was sure the neighbours would complain.

So she decided to move Pasha to the study, close the windows and turn on the air-conditioning in the hope that the dog would eventually stop barking incessantly.

"I think she was scared and still looking for her mother. That first night, she barked even when we sat with her. And she barked non-stop for at least a week. It was always such a wrench to leave her at home and go to work."

With subsequent visits to the vet, and armed with a general all-clear, Michelle focused on clearing her pup's skin issues and scheduling her vaccinations.

Toilet training was the next thing as Pasha had the study to herself all day. That was hard work. Her hooman was still working full-time so she had to find effective solutions. The vet had suggested the use of pee trays which she would use inconsistently. That meant the study needed to be mopped every evening. Along the way, both owner and dog discovered that they were allergic to Dettol floor cleaner!

Leash training took some time. Michelle started out using a harness as the young pup liked to escape her collar. When she grew bigger, and on the advice of dog walkers that they met at Bishan Park, Michelle decided to take her to doggy school. Pasha was pulling on her leash all the time and she had no clue how to deal with that. Pasha turned out to be a quick learner but also a headstrong dog with a mind of her own.

Their trainer thought Pasha might be a Belgian Shepherd mix, and his business partner confirmed it. They both gave good advice on how to handle her – be firm or she would take advantage, don't use a harness as she needed a Martingale and would respond better. She would learn fast and always remember but training was going to be an ongoing business so Michelle had to handle her consistently. And both pointed out that training isn't just for the dog but for the owner as well. We have to teach the dog how to survive in our world, understand our needs and expectations, and, vice versa, owners must be trained to understand their dog's needs, to read their signals and speak their language.

"I think that the one thing we all don't realise is that doggy school isn't for the dogs but for the humans. So that we can better understand our dogs and learn how to work with our dogs so that they in turn can understand what we want from them."

Diet was another challenge. Pasha seemed to react to certain food groups so it was through a process of elimination, coupled with all sorts of advice and suggestions from well-meaning friends that Michelle managed to figure out what worked and what didn't.

Travelling became a two-stage logistics endeavour. Michelle needed to travel extensively for work, and, with practice, had the science of packing for both down pat. First, she would pack for Pasha and make sure that her parents had everything they needed for the dog's homestay. Then she would do her own packing for travelling.

"It's like having a child!"

Pasha is a classic Shepherd. She sticks close to her human and always faces forward to scan the horizon.

"I always wondered if she remembered anything from doggy school and amazingly, she needs few spoken commands to sit, stand or walk. A gentle tug of the leash and she does what she needs to do."

Time flies when you're having fun, and Pasha has gotten older. And, with age comes health complications.

Pasha was diagnosed with hip dysplasia sometime in 2013 and had surgery to address the problem. She also has a wonky left knee.

"Her recovery was always going to be a lengthy process as her first instinct when she was more mobile was never to put any weight on her right leg. The vet and I had finally figured out something that could work when she tore the ligament in her left knee and went in again for another operation to correct that issue. It really was huge heartache for me as each time you put your furkid under GA, it is a worrying experience.

After the second surgery we had to work with a physiotherapist to help Pasha regain the strength in her hind legs and hips. It's been a long road. We took eighteen months of swimming, massages and slow walks to get her back to strength. And she was also growing older along the way. While she no longer has the speed and power she had as a younger dog, and she's getting a little arthritic now, Pasha remains mobile. She still runs around at my Mum's place and she still enjoys her walks. They may be a little shorter and a little slower now, but nothing beats the peace of a quiet walk – just Pasha and me.

PASHA WITH AUNTIE MARION,
MISS SINGAPORE UNIVERSE 1987

high threshold, so the vet monitors her, and her hooman has learnt to read the behavioural signs. It's a commitment. When you decide to welcome that dog into your life, you accept all the responsibilities that come with it, warts and all. And you fight old age together. People who abandon their senior or sick dogs are really just cowards taking the easy route. Dogs are unconditional in their non-judgemental love, and we should reciprocate.

Pasha has seen the family through times of loss and huge sadness, and she always seems to instinctively know when a hug is needed.

"My dog has been there for me through some really tough times. Her unconditional love has helped me get through a lot. Life has changed a great deal for me and for our family. These dogs worm their way into your heart and it's hard not to worry about them.

These days, I enjoy coming home to a quiet space and furry brown ball of love, hugs and snuffles. Nothing beats a quiet evening at home – just me and my princess dog. I read, she snoozes away. And all seems right with the universe.

What could be better than that?

Pasha is my first dog ever. And I'm happy with that. We don't need designer dogs. A dog is a dog and they will love you no matter what. And they remain loyal until the day they die. Those things are beyond a price tag.

Would I do it all again? Yes. Pasha has been worth every effort – she loves unconditionally and her loyalty is unwavering. I can't imagine life without her in it or the joy of that silly ball of fur leaping around excitedly when I get home each day."

And she has monthly cartrophen injections to help with the arthritis, as well as daily doses of joint support tablets and cod liver oil. Her back is also getting arthritic and she now takes Neurobion to help relieve the ache in the spine.

It's getting harder for her to walk so she wears braces for both knees all the time now when we are out as it helps her get up and move around comfortably. Part of it is due to the fact that the muscles around the hip are shrinking. It is all part of the aging process and I'm trying to figure out what would work for her so that she is comfortable.

As she gets older, I worry about how she will manage with walking. We've been lucky to find a wonderful vet and a wonderful physiotherapist who take care of her and provide sound advice on how to look after her as she ages."

Michelle is constantly asked how much she spends on her dog. Pasha goes for a blood test and ultrasound once a year. It's costly, but it's necessary. Dogs cannot articulate their pain and often have a

#TwistOfFate

Some people are just destined to connect.

Perhaps it was the Gods who engineered the crossing of paths between Anna and Elliott. Call it fate or fluke, but it was a match that was meant to be.

"I lost four dogs in 2015. They all left me due to old age or illness. Three of them were mine and the fourth was a foster but I loved them all equally. It was a rough year. These were my fur kids and they have all been with me for a very long time – from 8 to 17 years. I told myself that I will not allow any more fur kids into my life as every departure is so painful. I had two foster fur kids left and I will see them thru their life time. That was my promise to them.

A few months later, I got a message from a friend to check out a Facebook link she'd sent me. There was a dog available for adoption that she thought I'd like. No more additional dogs, I insisted, and we left it at that.

A few weeks later, I visited the same friend at her shop and she showed me a clip of a dog with a broken hind leg that had been left untreated since he was a puppy. I was really upset that someone could leave a poor puppy to suffer with a broken leg and not bother to treat it. I saw how he walked and understood his discomfort. I was full of anger but somehow, sadness overtook my emotions. I agreed to see him.

I did not realise that this was the same dog that was up for adoption on Facebook! We went to the shelter and waited for the keeper to come through the gate with him. Within a couple of minutes, this exuberant boy came charging into the compound and ran towards me. He bombarded me with loads of wet kisses. It was as if he knew that I was there for him.

He was only a-year-and-a-half but he had been living in the shelter for about a year. I could not bring myself to walk away and leave him there to spend the rest of his life at the shelter. He was so young and already, he had spent more than half his life there, suffering with a deformed leg.

I wanted to help him. I wanted to give him a chance to heal and to be able to use his leg normally like a regular dog.

I decided I was going to take Posh home, and immediately renamed him Elliott, a name that means Brave and Truthful. So much more appropriate for him than a flaky, pretentious name like Posh!

He kept wagging his tail the whole way home and had a smile on his face. He was curious about everything and explored every inch of the house. I dare say it was the happiest I'd seen him since I laid eyes on him.

He got along well with my home dogs. They are so used to having new dogs join the pack, as I was always fostering, so they accepted him easily and he fitted in quite well.

Many of my dogs were adopted, and I have fostered many others, so I am used to the baggage that they bring along. But Elliott was different. He was very young, and had spent most of his life locked up at the shelter so he had no notion of life in the real world. He had no training to speak of, nor was he socialised with other dogs so he was completely clueless with not much etiquette to boot. He sucks up food like a vacuum cleaner and doesn't understand the command 'wait'. He is not a fussy eater and will grab any food from your hand. You may even find your fingers in-between his teeth occasionally!

Despite all that, he is absolutely the sweetest boy. He would sit by you and put his head on your lap; he would give in to his older sister when she wants the toy that he has; he is very protective of us. He is a boy that stays away from trouble. All he wants is to be loved and fed, which he receives in abundance.

We have also tried to address the issue of his leg as best we can. He has seen a couple of vets and a specialist as well as an orthopedic surgeon. He is coping well at the moment, with short walks and regular swimming sessions, but we know that problems will arise when he gets older, so we need to prepare him for that day when it comes.

I have had dogs all my life. They have each impacted and influenced me at different stages of my life, and in different aspects of my work.

Little John was an English Cocker Spaniel who lived to the ripe old age of 17 ½. I took him everywhere with me and we had a great bond. We participated in agility obedience trials, pet therapy, training and lots of doggie activities, and he was very well socialised. He was the dog that has inspired and shaped the work I do today.

When I had Gigi, a Shiba Inu, I learnt all about the breed and realised just how intelligent they are. Before I started Hydro Paws Plus, I worked as a dog trainer after I returned to Singapore upon getting my certification in New Zealand. I used to volunteer at the Singapore Kennel Club as a trainer for their AVA and SPCA approved 'Good Canine Citizen' programme. I was also very heavily involved in training rescues and rehomed dogs. Gigi was the one dog who challenged me constantly during training and helped me grow as a dog trainer.

I adopted Diesel when he was two. His owner was leaving the country and had no interest in taking his goldie along with him. Diesel had the sweetest temperament. He was a giving dog who was brimming over with love for his humans. Diesel taught me how unconditional a dog's love is, and how shallow some humans can be.

My fourth dog was a Shar Pei, rescued from a farm. She had been chained up with a rusty chain in an algae-and-moss infested room that was constantly damp and dirty. When she was rescued, she had major skin issues, which I had to learn to control. When I started fostering her, she was rather aloof, but as time passed and we got to know each other, her playful side began to emerge. The poor girl never got a chance to play during her growing up years, so we tried to make up for it. We decided to adopt her eventually, and named her Aunty Dorothy. She passed on at 13.

I started Hydro Paws Plus in 2010. I realised, in the course of working with the many varieties of dogs, that there were many with orthopaedic issues. There were also a fair number of them who were overweight. I started to research effective therapy techniques, and ended up getting certified in hydrotherapy in the UK and US.

Over the course of the nine years (and close to 10,000 swims!) since I've started hydrotherapy, I have grown to love many of the dogs that have stepped through my doors. Losing one of them to the rainbow bridge is as painful as letting my own dogs go. It is really difficult. Every single one of them is special. My only consolation with my own four babies is that they left peacefully at their own time.

Elliott is still young but I know that day will come when I will have to say goodbye to him too. My aim is to give him as comfortable and safe a life as I possibly can, filled with love. I am mum to him and he is manja with me. I am enjoying every single moment with him, and he has become a wonderful companion.

"

The hubs and I have very different work schedules. Meredith fills in
the gaps when we are apart and sweetens the times when we are together.

"

GLENDA CHONG

#UptownGirl

Meredith is a beautiful long haired ex-breeding Weimaraner that was rescued from an illegal breeder and bailed out from the pound on Valentines Day of 2017. She's statuesque, chic and regal with a strong Patrician profile, juxtaposed against a quirky, madcap personality.

Glenda and her husband Justin were at a pet café within the grounds of the doggie day care, having tea with the founder of an

AWG one Sunday afternoon. The conversation at the table segued to cute puppies, and Glenda mentioned that Weimaraner pups were adorable because of their blue eyes. The founder asked if they would like to see Meredith.

They both nodded enthusiastically in unison.

The girl was brought out and she headed straight for Justin. It was almost as if she knew whose heartstrings to tug at.

"Up to that point I'm pretty sure he was skeptical but after going on a little jaunt with her around the compound and playing some ball, I knew his heart was stolen. Maybe vice-versa too!

I was still hesitant about adopting another dog as I had lost my best friend, Pinto, a Wire Fox Terrier, just a year ago. He died of old age and I still miss my companion terribly. He was my dog and I had him 14 years ago, long before I married Justin. Pinto was my darling."

Meredith was friendly but shy. But it was obvious she liked Justin and Glenda.

"Justin was giving me the look, something I've learnt to interpret as 'I want'. I looked at Meredith, gave her a treat and realised she has the gentlest mouth. She doesn't snatch food from your hands. I knew that Justin was smitten and we decided to adopt Meredith as our dog. You see, Pinto was my dog and not really our dog so Meredith would be ours."

Glenda and Justin decided to pick Meredith up the next day, as they had to prepare the home for her arrival.

"Luckily, Terry Peh from Good Dog People was also present when we first met Meredith and he arranged for everything to be sent to our place. You can say we were there at the right time, right place and it was just meant to be."

Meredith was brought home on a Sunday. She was, as expected, apprehensive but curious of her new surroundings, as all dogs would be.

"The first thing we did when we got home was take her for a little walk around the compound. The hubs (who completely hates taking pictures) said 'Wait! I need to get a photo of my two models.' Where I've failed in getting him to take pictures, Meredith succeeded without even trying!!!"

Meredith settled in really quickly. They took about two weeks to toilet train her, and put her through one obedience class. It was pretty much smooth sailing for the three of them.

The couple also discovered Meredith's taste for the finer things in life!

"One day, we found that she had managed to help herself to some imported salami from the kitchen counter. We didn't realize how tall she was as our previous dog was tiny.

She has also developed a taste for (the French designer shoe label) Louboutins! Of all the shoes in my shoe rack, she knew which was the most expensive! I've since taken to hiding all my shoes."

Glenda and Justin got a doggy gate and tried to confine her in the kitchen when they were out, but *"she started making noises like she was being tortured. So we decided to gave her free reign to the entire house. Except the bedrooms. That was off-limits. I was also adamant that she not be allowed on our bed.*

I came home one day to find my husband sound asleep on the bed with Meredith next to him. He was using the dog as a bolster. We bought a doggie bed for her but she now prefers to sleep with us in our bed.

So much for off-limits!

Our nights have, however, now become much cozier."

Meredith soon became a big hit amongst all of Glenda's and Justin's friends. As most of Glenda's colleagues were investigative journalists, they soon dug up the story of Meredith's past.

"Some of our google gifted friends did some snooping and there she was on our CNA website!"

According to a CNA report dated 17 May 2017, a 39-year old woman, Lin Xiaoqun, a Singapore permanent resident, had been charged in court in May 2017 with keeping a dog farm illegally and breeding dogs without a license. Her nine adult dogs and four puppies, were voluntarily surrendered to the authorities. The adult dogs, including Meredith, were used for breeding and they were unlicensed.

"She was little then but there was no mistaking that face staring back at us from the article was our gorgeous little rescue."

Meredith was one of the very lucky ones to have been rescued from a horrific life at a young age. Many breeding dogs are not so lucky.

"Meredith has brought so much love to us. She completes our home.

Meredith is affectionate, endearing, clumsy but most of all vocal. It's almost like having a talking dog. She enjoys grumbling the most and we've since nicknamed her Grumbilina. She especially reserves her grumbles for the hubs. She is the only person who can get away with nagging him!

Both the hubs and I grew up with dogs and they were all loved but this is the first dog that we own together. We try to be the best pawrents we can be - patient , loving and not overly attached to our shoes."

#EasterPups

It was certainly a Good Friday in 2012 for Asher and Astro. They, along with their four other siblings, were found by independent rescuers at Yishun Dam. The two-month-old pups had almost drowned due to the high tide but were finally trapped and rescued on Easter Sunday.

Their saviours began immediately to look for fosterers and adopters for the pups.

Jamie and her sister had always wanted a dog since they were young, but their parents felt they weren't ready. Only when the four siblings finally grew up, and dad and mom felt they were old enough to take responsibility for their four legged charge did they finally give the green light. Now that the time was right, Jamie's sister began scouring the internet for dog adoption sites.

"My sister has always had a heart for animals since she was young, and researched extensively about dog ownership and the dog trade. When we were ready for a dog, she educated us about puppy mills and why we should adopt instead. So we decided our dog was not going to come from a pet shop"

As fate would have it, she chanced upon a Facebook post by a rescuer friend of hers. The title "Easter pups" intrigued her. It was an adoption notice for Asher, Astro and their siblings. The two sisters fell in love with the picture of Asher and contacted the rescuers immediately to register their interest in the pup.

"We had only intended to adopt one dog, being first time pet owners."

A home visit was arranged and all five puppies were brought to meet our family. (It was most unfortunate that one of their siblings had passed away by then, due to a maggot wound.)

ASHER
ASTRO

The puppies were sleeping in their carriers when they were first brought to our home by the rescuers. It was love at first sight when we laid eyes on puppy Asher but another puppy soon wormed his way into our hearts too. We sat around the puppies and as they began to warm up, Astro (then known as Arley) came up to me and slept on my lap. It felt as though it was he who chose us and wanted us to be his family. At that moment, little Astro completely ran away with our hearts. Puppy Astro was way too cute to resist and we decided to adopt both Asher and Astro."

When it was time for the adoption, Asher and Astro were picked up from their fosterer's home by Jamie and her sister.

66

We take our hats off to the passionate and devoted rescuers who dedicate their lives to the rescue of strays, abused, neglected and chained dogs and the like. It is a never-unending job that is sometimes met with hostility, abuse and indifference. They risk life and limb for the sake of the dogs, often relying on donations and the goodwill of others when their own well of savings dry up. Our family is ever so grateful to the team that rescued Asher, Astro and their siblings.

99

JAMIE FWAH

"They were so small that we could carry them in our arms throughout our ride home. They slept throughout the entire journey, nestled in our arms. Puppies Asher and Astro officially became members of our household on the night of 2 May 2012."

Being first-time dog owners, Jamie relied on her basic knowledge as well as the research she and her sister had done prior to the adoption to care for the pups.

"It was chaotic. We were trying our best to raise the pups well but it was all trial and error. Every single day was an adventure with them and we grew and learnt together.

We puppy-proofed the house, bought them beds, blankets, toys, bones et al to get them to be as comfortable as they could. My sister did all of the research and was in charge of toilet and leash training as well as all medical issues. She kept a diary on what the pups did and ate and even the times they pooped daily.

find. Table legs, chairs, shoes, newspapers, painted walls, toilet rolls, letters and parcels were all destroyed. Fences built to puppy-proof the house were all bitten and destroyed. The fences were repaired and changed so many times that their contractor eventually gave them a discount!!!

We were overly protective of the pups and thought that they could only go outdoors to socialise when they were fully vaccinated. Hence, we missed their critical stage of socialising at six months. They were more afraid of people and loud sounds then but through desensitization over time, Asher and Astro are better now."

The boys were also fond of digging. It was a losing battle trying to cover all the holes, as new ones would appear twice as fast as they were being filled. Flowers, plants and vegetables that were planted in the garden were uprooted as well.

Puppyhood was an absolutely crazy experience for all parties.

Leash training was another challenge. Going on walks seemed like a constant battle. The pups would pull and tug and react throughout a 30-minute walk. The boys fought for dominance throughout puppyhood, which proved to be rather stressful for the family.

Being first-time owners, Jamie and her sister ended up overfeeding the boys. They were worried that they might not have enough nutrients. The dogs ended up having diarrhoea most of the time and were brought to the vet ever so often. They eventually found out that it was because they had too much nutrients in their diet. Asher and Astro ended up with huge food bellies.

As the dogs approached adulthood, Jamie was faced with a new set of problems, the most disturbing of which stemmed from her fellow humans.

And then there was toilet training. The sisters would wake up in the morning to find smeared poop and pee all over the house. It took months before the boys were toilet trained.

"We faced discrimination at the start when the boys were old enough to go to public places, like parks and cafes. 'So big, looks so fierce, they will sure bite' were some of the nasty comments we would get from people.

Jamie also had to content with teething. The boys would chew on anything they could

These were often accompanied by disgusted looks. There was also the issue of other dog

owners who tried to impose their methods on me. Maybe it was because I was a girl with two big dogs. Not everything that works on your dog will work with others. We've met owners who've screamed in the boys' faces or tried to lay their hands on them, in an attempt to 'correct' their behaviour. And there are others who allow their off-leash dogs to just run up to our boys without asking. Not all dogs are comfortable being approached in this manner, especially when my boys are on leash. But many dismiss it with an 'Oh, my dog doesn't mind!'. Yeah, but MY dogs do!

Getting transport was especially difficult when we had to go out because they were big. And I had not one but two big dogs!"

There was also a problem with their food. The dogs were fed a special diet which wasn't readily available in Singapore.

"We did all the research we could, sourcing for the right food even if it costed more. We also had to make sure the pups would have enough nutrients. We fed the best quality food and multi-vitamins we could find. It didn't help that the boys were picky with food, so it was a challenge to source for a variety of different foods to add to their meals. When the boys were older, we also started them on home-cooked food.

We read up on stories online of people who placed their dogs on similar diets and how their pets thrived on it. Those stories helped us a lot."

Asher and Astro have grown into two different dogs with completely different personalities.

Asher is the gentle giant, always in his own world. His favourite activity is to just lie alone and watch the world go by.

"All the way through puppyhood till he became one, we were almost convinced he was a deaf dog because he wouldn't respond whenever we called his name. Plus, he never barked."

He has also a kind heart, coupled with a silly sense of play.

"When he was still a puppy, he chased a chameleon around the house and eventually caught it with his mouth, we thought he was going to eat it but he let the chameleon go after playing with it."

When it's bath time at home, he goes into 'play dead' mode because he knows the girls are not strong enough to lift him off the floor!

Astro, by contrast, is the serious one. He is the self-appointed guard dog of the house and would alert the family should monitor lizards, monkeys, birds and other wildlife try to sneak into the house. He even has a different bark for animals and humans! He is the brother with the resting bitch face, who was nicknamed angry bird by his rescuers, but is, in reality, a gentle giant who is not capable of hurting even a fly.

Both of the boys have completely integrated themselves into the household and have even earned their keep.

"One day, my dad realised that Astro was barking non-stop for the longest time whilst standing on his hind legs looking over the fence which bordered our kitchen. He decided to check on Astro and found the kettle boiling over. My dad was boiling water and had forgotten all about it. Astro saved our home."

The boys are also very instinctive, and extremely protective of Jamie.

"I was out on my usual walk with the boys. They were walking behind me when they suddenly stopped. I turned around and saw Astro seated defensively. Both boys had their backs to me. I noticed at that point that there was a group of men who were following us. The boys had their eyes fixed onto the men and did not flinch. The men finally walked away."

Leia and the boys met at Hydro Paws Plus. Leia would peer over from her treadmill tank at Astro in between her sets and I would notice Astro sneaking glances at Leia whilst he was swimming laps in his pool. Asher, meanwhile, would wait patiently by the side of the pool for his turn. The three dogs would then turn the waiting area into their own little playground after their sessions and shower, stopping only for treats dispensed by 'Aunty Anna', the lovely owner.

"I was so depressed when Astro was diagnosed with arthritis. It is heart breaking to see him in pain at times, and we had to look for solutions to help him. I'm glad he is doing good with therapy now. Asher has seasonal allergies and there are times when the itch gets so bad that he scratches till he bleeds. We do our best to ease his discomfort."

I was really glad that, in Jamie and Anna, I had found people I could

> 66
>
> **Adopt don't shop. I hope people would open their hearts more to rescues/strays and understand them. Breeds don't define anything. Rescued/stray dogs aren't any less worthy of love and second chances than any other dogs.**
>
> 99

JAMIE FWAH

have meaningful discussions with about our dog's problems without being trolled or judged. We share the same fears, the same insecurities, the same doubts and the same questions. Our dogs suffer from the same orthopaedic ailments and allergies. What bonded us together was our unwavering love for our canines and the fact that we all adopted.

"A lot has changed after Asher and Astro entered my life. I've always been lacking in confidence. I needed a lot of courage to talk to people in the past, let alone initiating conversations. It was only after Asher and Astro came along and we started going on adventures together that I had the courage to be more sociable. Today I can initiate conversations with other dog owners and plan playdates with them. Asher and Astro have helped me to be more confident and showed me how to be responsible, how to forgive and how to love. They've filled our home with so much love, laughter and happiness, so it's only right that we do the best we can and go that extra mile for them and love them like family."

"

We can judge the heart of a man by his treatment of animals.

"

IMMANUEL KANT

SHOT ON LOCATION
@
WHEELER'S ESTATE

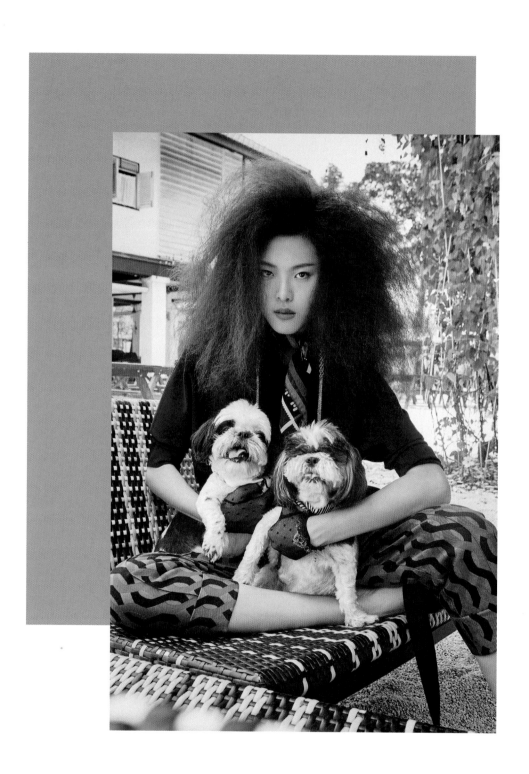

"

'Rescue'
does not mean
'damaged'
It means they
have been
let down by
humans.

"

#JustTheTwoOfUs

There were 25 dogs in the runway show. Most of them strutted up and down the catwalk to rapturous applause. Booboo, however, thrilled the audience when she appeared and started to perform party tricks on stage. The exuberant dog looked like she led a charmed life but it was no walk in the park. According to her adopters Janice and April, *"it took a long time and a lot of patience to get to where we are today"*.

Booboo was the youngest of a litter of seven pups, the result of an accidental pregnancy. Her mom belonged to a relative of her pawrents, who asked to adopt one of the pups when they heard about the pregnancy.

"Booboo was our very first dog so we started off as very inexperienced pawrents. She came home to us when she was two months, right after she was weaned from her mother.

At six months, we got a home trainer in to teach us how to potty train Booboo as well as instill basic discipline in her. He told us during the very first lesson that we will have to let Booboo know we are her leaders as she is a very smart dog. She can be manipulative and will assert her position in the household.

Alas, as the soft-spoken and kind-hearted one in the household, I was never able to get her to obey me. I was also pretty busy at work and was seldom home to spend time with her.

In retrospect, I don't really think I had much of a relationship with her during her first year with us."

There was more drama. When they let their guard down occasionally when the front door was open, Booboo would escape. The more they chased, the faster and further she would run. It was pretty dangerous as the front door led straight to the road.

April decided to bring her for group obedience training. Janice was still too busy and pretty much sat out of the training. April spent many hours practising with Booboo outside of training, and eventually, she passed her Good Canine Citizen test after eight weeks. However, she was still far from being a consistently obedient dog. She was constantly barking; she would lunge at other dogs during walks and her recall was bad!

Janice and April decided to enrol her in agility classes next. In such courses, the owners and their dogs run as a team to complete a designated course. Janice decided to participate with her dog.

"It was strikingly obvious that Booboo and I lack team spirit and communication. It wasn't surprising at all since I did not have much of a relationship with her, but I didn't understand that back then. I was always angry and frustrated with her whenever she decided to take things into her own paws and run her own course instead of following my cues. Classes were no fun because of the constant frustration with each other and it only put a further strain on our relationship (or lack thereof)."

66

Having a dog is pretty much like having a kid. You need to put in the time to nurture them. This is especially so for dogs with temperaments that are not naturally mild or those with a higher energy level. So many people cite the lack of time and the inability to handle their dogs as reasons for giving them up. So many of these dogs end up with the raw end of the deal through no fault of their own. These dogs really deserve better and deserve a second chance at life.

99

JANICE & APRIL

Janice decided to rectify the situation. With advice from trainers and lots of online research, she started to bring Booboo on weekly expeditions to explore different parts of Singapore. They would also join friends and their dogs for pack walks and visit dog-friendly events with her. In doing so, they exposed her to different environment, people and situations while spending quality time together. All these helped the two girls bond and Booboo has become calmer as a result of it. She is able to control her impulse better and has become a pretty confident dog. They continued with the agility classes and did so well, Booboo won her first agility trophy three days shy of her second birthday!

"I'm so glad I didn't just call it quits when the going got tough. I see many people giving up when they realise that reality does not match their perceived fantasy of their ideal dog. Not many people are willing to put in that hard work and invest the time at building that relationship. Instead, the dog is, more often than not, left to their own devices, neglected by their owners. Some owners take the cowardly way out and abandon or give them up eventually."

The girls started looking forward to classes every weekend, but decided to call it quits on the competition front.

"We stopped bringing her for competition when we realized she was stressed by all the other competitor dogs barking incessantly. She was always falling sick right after each competition."

Because dogs need mental stimulations as much as physical activity, Janice signed Booboo up for trick classes. She has also started participating in dog parkour, where the animals navigate obstacles found in their natural environment. This sport has allowed Booboo to spend even more quality time with Janice in a fun and energetic way."

Booboo and I are now inseparable and we read each other's body language pretty

(L-R)
BOOBOO, HAPPY

well. I'm proud to say we have a strong relationship today. Booboo's confidence level has also increased by leaps and bounds.

We were so encouraged by her progress, because of the time we invested in her, the patience to build a relationship and to understand her, it has all paid off. All dogs are good dogs; they just need to learn how to live in our world and by our rules, and humans need to be trained to help them. Learning is a lifelong process for both"

A couple of days before she turned two, Booboo passed her temperament test and officially become a member of Therapy Dog Singapore (TDS). She has also been accepted into the Healing Paws therapy programme by SOSD and started her own therapy dog journey with the Assisi Hospice.

All the tricks she learnt have come in really useful in her role as a therapy dog. She uses them to amuse the residents of the homes she visits, and to break the ice with those who are afraid of dogs.

Early in 2018, Janice and April decided they were ready to give Booboo a companion. They decided to adopt so that they could give a needy dog that second chance at life.

In December 2017, two dogs were put up for 'sale' on Carousel. Their ex-owners gave an ultimatum – either pay the price or they would be sent to AVA to be put down.

A kind lady saw the post and rescued them that very day. She brought the two dogs home with her and cared for them for a couple of months whilst looking for a forever home for them. She was not able to keep them herself as she already had three dogs.

"I had just landed in Singapore when I saw a Whats App message in one of my chat groups; it was an adoption notice for Happy and her sister. I decided there and then to enquire about Happy, and did so even before I stepped out of the airport. There was something about Happy that drew me to her. Call it love at first sight if you will."

Janice had to wait a week before she got a reply. The fosterers' priority was to rehome the less independent of the two dogs, who was rather attached to Happy. She was eventually rehomed in January and the girls were finally allowed to meet Happy.

On 3 February 2018, Booboo and her pawrents met Happy at a pet café. The two dogs were surprisingly comfortable with each other, and sat quietly whilst the hoomans had their lunch. There was no snapping, no barking and no cattiness. The girls were also able to touch and carry Happy. They decided to give Happy her forever home.

"We went to pick Happy up from the fosterer's home a week later, on 10 February 2018. According to the fosterer, she had told Happy that she will be going to her forever home that day. The fosterer, her helper and her neighbour brought Happy down to meet April, Booboo and I. We chatted for a while at the void deck and when it was time to say goodbye, Happy went to all three of them individually to bid her farewell, and then she followed us away without looking back. It was a sight I can never forget. It's like she understood what was exactly happening that very day.

On her first night with us, Happy just followed us quietly around the house, never letting us out of her sight. Her fosterer had given us the bed she was sleeping on the past three months, as well as her toys. We set her bed next to ours and put her toys out, in case she felt homesick, but she wanted nothing to do with them. When it was time for bed, she ignored hers and jumped onto a small ottoman nearby and settled in. She was happy just to be near us.

We were afraid to let her into our bed the first night, for fear of Booboo feeling threatened. However, we woke in the middle of the night and carried her into our bed. We were afraid she might be cold from the air conditioning, which was right in front of the ottoman. The night passed peacefully with nary an incident."

Happy settled in pretty quickly and got used to the routine at the house. With time, she got her groove back and started to become more confident.

"When she first come to us, Happy was a pretty quiet dog. We did not hear her bark at all until about a month into the adoption. But she had a really loud and shrill whine and would spin around excitedly whenever we took out the leash. We had to train her to calm down."

Along with her newfound confidence, she also found her voice.

"She started barking at every sound and movement outside the house. She would bark at visitors. She would also bark at unfamiliar people when she was visiting our friends or relatives. As long as she was indoors, she would bark! I guessed (perhaps wrongly) that it was a sign of being territorial. After a while, we figured that her constant barking in our home environment or in places she deemed to be safe seemed to stem from her sense of insecurity. She was probably afraid that those unfamiliar faces were coming to take her away from us. We are not sure how many homes she had been shuttled to and fro, but it would have been a very traumatizing experience for her. This time round, after feeling secure and happy with us, she was probably as afraid of losing us as we are of losing her. We also realized that she would not allow anyone other than us to carry her out of the car. On several occasions, when a friend would attempt to help us, Happy would cling on desperately and not let go.

Her constant indoor barking is not to be encouraged and we are trying to teach her to stop. We have a long way to go but we can see a slight improvement.

Outdoors, she's still a pretty quiet dog. But her confidence has led her to be as stubborn as Booboo now; she has a mind of her own too and wants to dictate where she wants to go when we are out for walks. She will stay rooted strongly or plant her butt on the ground and not budge if we don't give in to her!"

Like a puppy seeing the world for the first time, Happy had to overcome her fear of walking beside a busy road. She had to learn how to ascend and descend stairs and jump up and down from the sofa and bed. She had to learn how to estimate the height of objects and how much energy she needs to propel her upwards. She had to be taught how to run!

"A lot of things she couldn't do in the past stemmed from a lack of exposure. It's never too late or too old to teach a senior dog new behaviour or new tricks as long as safety is not compromised. Happy is still afraid of thunder and lightning but all she needs is her butt against yours and she feels safe. If we happen to be out during a thunderstorm, Happy will find comfort in Booboo; she will lie beside her to feel safe."

Happy's ex-owner was not very forthcoming with her history so Janice and April did not know much of her past life. They decided to send her for a comprehensive medical checkup.

An ultrasound scan picked up an ugly and scarily massive tumour in her spleen. During her second month in her new home, she underwent a major surgery to prevent her spleen from rupturing, which would have been life threatening. Happy's spleen was removed in its entirety and sent for biopsy.

Nothing, it seems, could get this wonderful girl down and she was bouncing up and down the day after her surgery, with no loss in appetite. It was almost like she was in a hurry to catch up on all that she had missed in the past eight years.

When the girls got the results, they discovered that Happy had histiocytic sarcoma, a very aggressive form of cancer. On a mitotic scale, more than 9 will indicate a shorter survival time. Happy's was 14.

The advantage she had was the early detection, and the removal of the entire spleen. Thankfully, the tumor did not

repture. All subsequent untrasounds have been positive, and the girls are praying hard that it remains that way.

"With Happy's condition, there are so many uncertainties surrounding us but we vowed to make one thing a constant – to let Happy lead as normal a life as happily as possible. It's been barely a year since Happy come to us and there are still so many things we would like to do with her. I'm sure the feeling is mutual. Happy has shown us what a feisty little fighter she is, she will not let adversity gets in her way; she is always positive and happy like her namesake."

Happy was originally named Apple. The girls decided to change the dog's name because the girl is just full of optimism and radiates happiness every single day.

"Every morning, when she wakes, the first thing she will do is to walk up to me and lick my face. When I finally open my eyes and greet her 'good morning', she will literally throw herself into my embrace and stay there for awhile, with her face buried in my neck or face. When I am preparing her breakfast, she will roll on the floor happily with the toy in her mouth. It's always a happy way to start a brand new day!"

Before Happy was adopted, the girls were inundated with many discouraging stories of second dog failures, of how the first dog got depressed, fell ill or acted up badly when a second dog entered the household.

"We were worried about how Booboo will react, as she has been an only child for four years, with all our attention focused on her. With Booboo's aloof, ice queen demeneour, we thought she was not capable of loving another dog. But time has proven us wrong. When Happy first come, they co-existed, each minding their own business. After a couple of weeks, I think it finally dawned on Booboo that Happy was here to stay for good. She wanted to dominate Happy by mounting her. Happy happily obliged (no pun intended!); she did not snap or bark her away.

We watched from the sidelines as they ironed things out themselves. Subsequently, we stopped Booboo from mounting Happy. But I think Booboo was happy that she had made her statement. She started to initiate play with Happy, who just stood there, confused. At that point, Happy had yet to learn how to respond to other dogs, not having socialized before.

One day, out of the blue, Happy finally responded by barking back at Booboo. Booboo gave chase, and they started playfighting.

These days, they will wrestle during playtime. Happy would always roll over into a vulnerable position for Booboo to play with her. This shows how confident and comfortable she is in her relationship with Booboo.

In the beginning, Booboo would resist any contact with Happy. As Happy did not have any sense of personal space. Booboo got stepped on and jumped upon. Booboo reacted by bolting. Today, both dogs can share the same doggy bed. Booboo would sleep next to Happy. She does not run away anymore. Slowly but surely, we can sense the building of a bond between the two dogs.

There was a time after Happy's second operation, while she was still recovering, when she tried to get Booboo to play with her. Booboo just walked quietly away. She seemed to understand that Happy had not fully recovered from her procedure and decided to let her rest.

The attention and time spent on Booboo was significantly reduced especially during the period before and after Happy's surgery, Booboo will get a little angsty at times but otherwise she was a pretty good sport. Many people have commented about how Booboo's disposition has softened since Happy came to us; she's more smiley and less aloof. We realised that too because she comes to us for hugs and cuddles more often now; in the past, Booboo was very particular about her personal space and resisted cuddles."

Happy has settled in with her sister and her pawrents most comfortably. She has also become a certified therapy dog with SOSD's Healing Paws and Assisi Hospice.

"With Happy and Booboo, it is always easy to know how much they love us, from the way they look into our eyes, the way they lick us all over to how they snuggle with us. Our dogs show their love very explicitly and generously and we love them back unconditionally in return. We would not want it any other way."

#HowCan YouMendA BrokenHeart

"Two years ago, I was asked to make a guest appearance on a television show with Desmond Tan. The premise of the show was – "how do you reach out to help a cause that you believe in, in 72 hours" We had the freedom to choose whatever causes we wanted. Desmond selected dog shelters, and suggested my name as a volunteer.

My heart started beating really fast when I heard this. I had been toying around for the longest time with the idea of keeping a dog, which my mother objected to. She passed away a few years ago and the house has been awfully quiet without her. The silence was deafening, and everyone was depressed.

I thought again of getting a dog. Now that my mom was not around, maybe this is the right time?

I knew I did not want to purchase one and toyed around with the idea of adoption. It wasn't something I was extremely serious about at that time, so I procrastinated.

When the show came along, I knew in my heart that I might come home with a dog.  MAN MAN

The shelter was at Pasir Ris. There were so many dogs there. They were smelly and many had health problems. Which one should I choose? Which ones would speak to me? I genuinely felt for all of them, but it wasn't possible to bring them all home.

I was given the option of adopting a three- or four-day-old black poodle puppy. Her mom was pregnant when they rescued her, and gave birth shortly after she arrived at the shelter. I looked at the puppies, and they were really cute, but I knew they were not for me.

As we continued to film, I took a stool and sat in their midst, enjoying their company. Some of the dogs came over to me. Then I spotted Man Man. It wasn't love at first sight, She was not the prettiest dog but something about her caught my attention. The other dogs were jumping around and up at me, stepping all over her and using her as a springboard to get to me. She didn't seem to mind at all. She just sat there, looking at me, calm and collected.

I wanted to get to know her better so the shelter encouraged me to take her home for a trial.

I remember putting a harness on her to take her for a walk, just to build rapport with her. She did not know how to react because she has never worn a harness before in her life. She literally froze on the spot. I also realized that all the different textures that we were walking on – concrete, stony, wooden, tiled etc – were alien sensations to her. She was an ex-breeding dog, locked in a cage all her life, so this was all new to her.

She never had a chance to see and experience the real world. It was heartbreaking to see that even something as basic as walking on the ground was a challenge for her.

When we got home, she started to roam around the house before falling off to sleep. She was like a different dog altogether. She was rigid and uptight at the dog shelter and very quiet, but the moment she set foot into the house, she started to prance around. I knew she enjoyed the space. She suddenly came to life.

She found a favourite place to sleep. I noticed that she was always sleeping with her face facing inwards, towards the wall. It was clear that she wasn't comfortable with facing human beings whilst at rest.

Man Man started to recover after some time. From a dog that was on the verge of death and suffering from all the health conditions that shocked even the vet, she has blossomed into a beautiful furball. We give her lots of love and care and she has thrived, a far cry from her days in the shelter when she was known as Patchy (because of her patchy fur). She has gone from this scrawny animal to a beautiful princess. It truly is a miracle.

Man Man is so calm that I am thinking of getting her trained as a therapy dog. People who meet her can see that she is different, and often ask if she was traumatized before.

I fell for Man Man partially because I wanted to give her a better life. When I looked into her eyes when we first met, I could see the sadness. She is so beautiful but with such a sad spirit. She was so broken inside. Dogs like her did not choose to be breeding dogs. It was just an unfortunate life they were born into.

People say that Man Man is so blessed to have found me. I would say that I am incredibly blessed to have found her. One dog with a broken heart meeting a human with a very broken past. It is such an interesting thought that we bring each other so much comfort. She has helped heal my heart and my soul. Life is suddenly better with her in my life, and I am ever so grateful.

I want to encourage all the people who want to get a dog to adopt. Never ever think that you are doing these abandoned or rescued dogs a favour. You will be surprised that they could be the ones doing you a huge favour by becoming your adopted pet, by becoming part of your family. You will never know how a rescue dog can change your life and can change the relationships that you have with your family. I never really spoke much to my dad till Man Man came into my life. Today, I have many conversations with him, and it often revolves around Man Man! My helper loves her dearly. She has brought us all together.

Love truly transforms hearts and lives. Love can heal broken hearts. I am much happier now because of Man Man. I embrace life to the fullest and have a more positive outlook on life. I have so much joy in my heart because of her.

I treat Man Man as an equal, like one of my own family. I give her unconditional love and grace and mercy. That's what we do for each other. Even when I am angry with her, she will still continue to love me and comfort me as though nothing has happened.

Man Man has taught me the power of forgiveness. She may only be an animal, yet she has the instinct and capacity to forgive me for my mistakes and accept me for my imperfections.

For that, I am eternally grateful."

#FosterFail

"We failed as fosterers," Cynthia said, with a wicked twinkle in her eye.

We were seated at Wheelers Estate, minders to our respective dogs that day as they preened and posed for a fashion shoot with professional models.

"We brought him to his first adoption drive, and there was no interest. My housemate, Ju, was so relieved that no one adopted him!" There were subsequent drives. Still no interest. Each time, Ju held his breath and prayed that Jnr would return to the home, pawrent-less.

After the umpteenth adoption attempt, and numerous heart-stopping, anxious 'Will Junior return? Oh please, let no one adopt him' moments, the housemates knew that he was there to stay."

Junior's fate – crossing paths with Cynthia – was written in the stars.

JUNIOR

"We were hoping to find my cat, Simba, a companion. Simba preferred to be in the company of dogs instead of other cats so I placed myself on SOSD's foster list. I had requested for older dogs but they told me that they had a four-month-old puppy that was an urgent case. From what I remember, Junior was already in foster care. I'm not sure why they could not continue to foster him.

When I first met him, he was a chubby fluff ball. We tried to guess his mix. He looked like he might have had a bit of German Shepherd in him. Over time, we concluded he looked more like a fox. Ha!

My housemates and friends were excited about Junior. He tested his welcome by eating our couch, my armchair, five pair of shoes, three pairs of expensive designer glasses amongst other things. I was furious. To this day, three little words, 'What is this?' is all it takes for him to know he'd been a bad boy.

Initially, Junior slept with Simba and I in my room every night. I fed him and walked him. I particularly enjoyed watching him play with Simba. However, I had to keep reminding myself that I was just fostering him and could not allow any attachment to form.

I took him to Bishan Park for his first adoption drive. There were no enquiries. When I took him home, my housemate Ju gave a whoop of joy! He was so happy to see him, glad that his adoption drive was a failure.

I can't remember exactly when Ju started to toy around with the idea of maybe keeping Junior. As much as I was tempted to consider adoption, I was realistic about my situation; I was planning to move to a different country so I'd only saved enough money to move Simba with me. I didn't think I was going to be able to afford to save enough money to move both the cat AND the dog!

Ju and I discussed it extensively. At the end of the day, we wanted to be responsible dog owners. Moving away is not an excuse to give up a pet.

I agreed we could keep him if Ju would adopt him legally. I would continue to love and care for him like my own. That's the sacrifice we make for our loved ones. I also made sure he was realistic about the time and effort it would take to look after a dog. Not once did he waver in his resolve to keep Junior with us.

And so here we are, foster fail!

We share the responsibilities and costs for Junior. These days, he sleeps with Ju in his room at night. But he still sleeps under my bed in the day. It is also his safe spot. If he feels threatened or wants to avoid being scolded, he will lay there. He has many other quirks too. He is very sensitive and very vocal as well. He likes to put his paw on my arm and my knee. He is very protective of me and of everyone especially when we are at home. He always barks outside my door in the morning to wake me up. He likes to sit on my lap. He loves head massages. He is very kissy and very licky. Squirrels are his nemesis. He gets very geram with the neighbours' dog so when he sees them, he will bite and shake the cushion on the sofa!

He loves bread, durian, yoghurt, mango and plain biscuits. His meals are lovingly prepared by CP, Ju's partner - brown rice with mince beef and mixed veggies, comprising carrots, corn and peas.

Junior has definitely helped to widen our social circle. We made a bunch of really great friends thanks to our dogs. We formed a playgroup for them. His best friends are Amber, a Golden Retriever and Lucy, a Singapore Special, both

also adopted. He doesn't get along well with unneutered dogs. Unfamiliar folks can't move too fast around him because it startles him. Unfamiliar folks cannot also move too slowly around him. He gets nervous wondering if you are plotting to do something to him. If he doesn't know you, you can't pet him, especially not on his head.

Junior is not my first dog. I grew up with dogs. But Junior is the first one I've had since puppyhood. My dogs and my cats were all adopted. I have loved each and every single one of them and they have, in return, loved me back a hundred fold.

Today, Junior is being cared for and loved by all five of us living under one roof."

It's really not difficult to be a good and responsible pawrent. Besides providing healthy food, clean water and plenty of exercise, a lot of patience and respect for your pet is needed. They are not property but family. They have feelings and they do bark, because that's how they speak. I also believe that it's the humans that should go for training to learn to handle their dogs better and to get a better understanding on how to read their pet's body language as well. Last but not least, give them lots of love and affection.

CYNTHIA LEE MACQUARRIE

#Touched
ByAnAngel

I know of adopters who seek out the oldest, sickest dogs with the most challenging special needs to adopt, with the aim of caring for them and allowing to live out the rest of their days in the cosy loving environment of a home. I salute these people and give them my utmost respect. It is something I have toyed around with, and I have fallen in love with so many of them. I want to take them home and care for them but I know I do not have the strength nor the emotional capability to do so.

Evan and Claudia are two such people. They are dog lovers who would open their hearts, their homes and their lives to the most needy and the most overlooked of dogs.

When they first approached the shelter, they said they were looking for a dog who had stayed in there for the longest time. They did not mind getting a senior dog or even one that was blind. These were issues that were the least important to them. All they wanted was to give that dog a second chance to be loved again.

The most crucial thing to them was that the newly adopted dog had to get along with their senior dog at home.

They were introduced to Navy, a senior dog who was blind and who had been in the shelter for the longest time. Navy was always overlooked at adoption drives because of her health and medical issues and also because of her age.

NAVY MUFFIN JUNIOR

She is typical of the sort of dogs who get left behind because many adopters come looking for younger, beautiful dogs to adopt.

But Navy certainly ticked all of Evan's and Claudia's boxes. They brought her home that very day.

(L-R)
MUFFIN, JUNIOR, NAVY

The couple have given Navy the best life she could've asked for; she gets all the love and attention she deserves; they bend over backwards to ensure she has the best medical support she requires. In short, they are dream adopters. Navy worked out so well for them that she was joined soon after by Muffin and Junior, dogs in situations similar to Navy.

According to Voices For Animals, *"Families like Evan and Claudia are the sort of adopters many of the rescue groups cherish. They come with the intention to help, and follow through on their promises. Their focus is not on the physical; their aim is to help the less fortunate, the ones with the broken souls, to give them the best second chance that they all deserve.*

Many people come for adoption drives hoping to get puppies or cute dogs and the senior ones get passed over. This mentality exists because they are under the (mistaken) notion that old dogs cannot learn new tricks. Some of them believe that a senior dog's life span is shorter and so they do not wish to invest in them."

That is sad. It is so fulfilling to help a dog on its last legs, ensuring they spend their final years in a loving home environment and letting them pass with dignity. Adopters like Evan and Claudia are truly angels who have touched the lives of the senior dogs they have welcomed into their lives.

#Sunshine AfterTheRain

There are many different types of adopters.

Some people go for adoption drives because they truly wish to help the animals. There are those who are knowledgeable about the reality of puppy mills, and prefer to get a pet through more humane methods. There are also those who turn up for adoption drives thinking it's a cheap (or free, god forbid!) way to get an animal.

And then there are those like June Tan.

I first heard of her when I started hanging out at the adoption drives to understudy the senior volunteers. Before each drive, pictures of some of the shelter dogs would appear on Facebook, perfectly groomed and photographed, to make them a little more presentable to potential adopters. I heard the name June mentioned several times but I only got to meet her when we rescued a poodle with a broken leg that had been thrown out of her house. *"Lets bring her to June. She has volunteered to groom her."* June spent the afternoon carefully combing through the mattered fur of this neglected dog before shaving her down and giving her a nourishing spa treatment to treat her scab-ridden and yeast-infected skin and manage the itch. And never took a cent.

Volunteers like June are a godsend and a great help to the animal welfare groups. She lends an invaluable helping hand to help keep the animals in good shape and looking good. After all, the first step in the healing process is looking and feeling good.

So it really came as no surprise when I discovered that June fosters and adopts the oldest, sickest, injury-ridden, health-plagued dogs that no one else would dream of taking a second glance at. She gives these dogs a second chance at life, and the oldest dogs knocking on deaths door a chance to experience the love of a home so that when they pass, they can do so with dignity.

I first met Grace and Hope when I went to her studio to pick up Kylie after a grooming session. I saw two beautiful dogs posing regally in the dog pen, minding their own business. Both dogs were adopted by June after she groomed them for their respective adoption drives. Deep down inside, she knew that it would be tough for these aged dogs to end up in a home, and embraced them instead.

"We were preparing for an adoption drive on 29 April 2017. It was only the second time we were working with the shelter and we decided to bring some of the dogs back to the shop as it would be easier to groom them on our premises. The plan was to let them stay over and we would send them to the drive the next day.

There were 12 dogs altogether, but only 11 were sent back. One of the dogs tugged so strongly at our heartstrings that we decided to keep her. We decided to call her Grace, which she responded to immediately, to our pleasant surprise.

Grace was born with deformed front legs and was blind in both eyes. We sent her to the vet for a through medical and discovered a brain tumor, which caused her to roll her eyes in a circular manner, as well as a tumor in her breast. She was also diagnosed with a slower heartbeat, almost half a second slower per minute.

Despite all her health problem, she was in amazing spirits and had a great appetite. And the most surprising of all was how she could constantly find her way to the pee pad to do her business despite losing the sight in both eyes!

We sent her to a specialist to remove her breast tumor in October 2018. It had grown to a worrying size and we thought it best to operate, although we were worried because of her advanced age and her heart condition, but the surgeon (who, coincidently, was the gentleman who performed the second TPLO operation on Leia) was confident. At the ripe old age of 13, Grace had her tumor removed.

HOPE

GRACE

Grace today is active and happy. She enjoys her car rides and will bark at us when it is time for her morning ride. We spoil her rotton and try to give her as best a life as possible.

Soon after Grace joined the family, we decided to take in another dog.

Hope was a dog we met when we volunteered out help for the very first time. The adoption drive was in February 2017, and Hope was one of the dogs we groomed. However, we sent her back to the shelter to try her luck.

Our paths crossed again in October 2017. I was shocked to see how much older she looked in the short span of eight months. All her four legs look weaker and she wobbled as she walked, although she was skinny.

She was, however, full of vigour and life and could not stay still during the post-grooming photo shoot. She was constantly asking for belly rubs, and really endeared herself to us.

We loaded the dogs into the van to bring them to the adoption drive, but we couldn't stop thinking about Hope. She managed to melt our hearts, and at the end of the day, 16-year-old Hope became the latest addition to our family"

"

I decided to adopt my two special needs dogs because I felt they were not suited for life in the shelter. I wanted to give them a comfortable home that they can spend the rest of their days. Although they are blind and have weak legs, there was really not much of a challenge taking care of them. They still manage to use the pee pad and lead life like normal dogs. They try to please us, even though they have special needs. I have learnt so much from them. They have taught me about unconditional love and how to always be positive. I have had absolutely no regrets adopting them.

"

JUNE TAN

SHOT ON LOCATION
@
CAPELLA SINGAPORE

> **"**
>
> *A dog is not a thing.*
> *A thing is replaceable. A dog is not.*
> *A thing is disposable. A dog is not.*
> *A thing doesn't have a heart.*
> *A dog's heart is bigger than any "thing"*
> *you can ever own.*
>
> **"**

ELIZABETH PARKER
PAW PRINTS IN THE SAND

> A lot of these dogs have a bad rep cos they are capable of hurting people and animals. Pit bulls, by nature, love people. Who's at the other end of the leash that can make the difference.
> It's about responsibility.

TIA TORRES

TIA TORRES IS THE FOUNDER OF VILLALOBOS RESCUE CENTRE AND THE STAR OF TV'S PIT BULL AND PAROLEES. SHE'S WORKED HARD TO CHANGE THE STIGMA THAT THERE IS ON PIT BULLS AND SHOW THAT THEY ARE INCREDIBLE ANIMALS FOR PEOPLE FROM ALL WALKS OF LIFE.

"

We don't care if we have her for three more years or three more days, we're going to make it the best life she's ever had. Sometimes I wonder if she remembers what it was like in the shelter, but I know she'd remember this forever.

"

JENNIFER HOYT

> Dogs, for a reason that can only be described as divine, have the ability to forgive, let go of the past, and live each day joyously. It's something the rest of us strive for.

JENNIFER SKIFF,
AUTHOR "THE DIVINITY OF DOGS:TRUE
STORIES OF MIRACLES INSPIRED BY MAN'S
BEST FRIEND

> "Until one has loved
> an animal, a part of
> one's soul remains
> unawakened.

ANATOLE FRANCE

251

❝

Keeping a dog requires a lot of commitment, responsibility, patience and time. Before you get one, keep in mind the various considerations like medical, diet and training. Are you financially ready? Research all you can about the breed, their health, their needs, suitable living conditions, appropriate diets and the like. Be aware of the food you're feeding them and don't buy into all that commercial hype. That's marketing.

❞

JOIE LEONG & YUJIN LIM

#HowOllieGot HisGrooveBack

Leia and Oliver met one sunny Sunday afternoon at Anna's. Leia had just completed her water treadmill session and Ollie was arriving for his. His papa YuJin and mama Joie are active volunteers at no-kill shelters and very passionate advocates of adoption.

"I started volunteering in 2008. The circle back then was very small and we had only just started using social media to create awareness for animal welfare. I remember posting an emotional tribute on facebook sometime in 2011 about missing my late silver blue poodle, Baby, who had passed recently at the grand old age of 18. I was contacted shortly after by a Facebook acquaintance asking if I was interested in adopting an abandoned blue poodle she had found on the streets. There had been absolutely no interest in the dog. It was hard then (and still difficult today) to get darker animals adopted, even a rare purebred.

OLIVER

I was very affected by the sudden death of my other poodle, Muffy, three years prior and I felt I could not bear to go through the heartache of losing another dog, especially since that death was followed by Baby's passing. This rescue reminded me so much of Baby; I told myself I wasn't ready but my husband YuJin was all for it. We decided to meet the dog for the first time on Valentine's Day.

I had such a strong feeling of guilt, as if I was betraying Muffy by accepting another dog into my life, but YuJin took to Ollie immediately. He was completely shaved down after his rescue so he did not resemble a poodle at all. He was scrawny, skittish and did not like to be touched. He was very very timid. I recognized these as obvious signs of being abused as well as survival traits he picked up, being on the streets on his own.

YuJin and I were a little nervous with this new commitment, and likewise, we sensed a feeling of apprehension in the dog. However, he fell asleep immediately in the car on the way home. He was either really comfortable with us or just exhausted from dealing with the drama of life.

When we got home, he ran to a dark corner and remained there, keeping very still and quiet. We decided to leave him there and warm up to his new home in his own time. We were entertaining friends at our home that evening, and his eventual godfather, Francesco, named him Oliver (after Oliver Twist).

Ollie took some time to adapt and to warm up to us. He would hide in his quiet corner and avoided contact with everyone. He would jump out of our arms if we tried to carry him. He was, however, enamoured by YuJin, who was the only one he would allow to carry him.

I spent more time with Ollie in his first month with us because I could bring him to work at the makeup studio. My flexible working hours also allowed me to work around the schedule we tried to establish for him. We worked out a routine for meals and walks. And discovered he could not function with an audience watching! He could only eat and drink when there was no one looking or when the lights were off. Likewise when he needed to do his business. He was really easy to train, though. In less than two months, he could eat in our presence and learnt to pop to his 'restroom' to relieve himself after every meal. Ollie's health was at the top of our agenda. We took him to the vet the morning after his adoption and were relieved to find out he had no major health issues. That joy did not last long. In his third month with us, we noticed cloudiness in one of his eyes. I suspected it was juvenile cataract but the vet disagreed. Fortunately, I wasn't entirely convinced and sought a second opinion. Thank goodness for intuition and gut feel. He ended up having his first cataract surgery. We also discovered his phobia of small, enclosed areas when we had to crate him at the clinic!

Ollie has since undergone a second cataract operation as well as femoral head osteotomy surgery.

Grooming sessions were extremely stressful for both Ollie and us because he does not like to be touched by humans. He is especially fearful of people holding on to his limbs and paws. After a long search and several stressful trial and error sessions, we finally found a groomer whose patience and low-stress techniques made such sessions possible. Ollie still visits the same groomer today.

It took Ollie the better part of 12 months but he eventually opened up. He no longer flinches when I hold on to his paws, and constantly yearns for our (not just YuJin's) company. He has evolved from a shy and timid dog to a confident alpha, comfortable with other dogs and able to keep order when the occasion calls for it.

We take him everywhere with us. We try to visit pet friendly cafes and bistros whenever we go out so he can be with us. We also realized how sneaky and naughty he could be. On one particular visit, he instigated and led a group of dogs at the café into the kitchen to steal food! We were alerted by a member of the staff and discovered a snaking line of dogs in the kitchen, led by our Pied Piper of a dog!

Ollie is brave, intuitive, intelligent, sensitive and loving. He knows no hatred. He has become very sociable and is very comfortable in huge crowds. He listens to instructions because he wants to please us, rewards notwithstanding.

He is the calmest dog we know, yet he is brave enough to stand up for himself when he needs to. He is really good with people and with other dogs. He is amazingly gentle with special needs dogs, especially those with disabilities. He assisted with the adoption of Toffee, a skittish, fearful poodle by keeping by his side and giving him reassurance. Toffee has since been adopted by my brother and mom and has grown into a crazy, confident, hyperactive dog!

Ollie has become a doggie celebrity of sorts, thanks to his presence on social media. Many people know Ollie by his name and we are just his humans. He is a social butterfly and attracts people to him like a moth to a flame. We have made so many new friends and reconnected with old ones through him.

When I have had a tough work day, I always feel relieved when I know that Ollie will be waiting at the door for me. Seeing him makes me forget about unhappy events of the day. Ollie's calmness and bravery during his several surgeries have definitely rubbed off on me. Whenever I get worked up, I think of him and that really calms me down. Suddenly, the dreadful dental or blood test which used to scare me seem a little better when I think of what he has gone through.

When Ollie came to our lives, we decided to give back as much as we could in his name. He was the lucky one who managed to find a home but there are many others who remain in shelters or on the streets. We have always been advocates of adoption and helping animals in need, but ever since the adoption, we started to actively create awareness on social media about animal shelters, puppy mills and breeding dogs. Buying from pet stores fuel the puppy mill trade. Demand for these puppies encourage the proliferation of irresponsible puppy mills where dogs are mistreated and live in appalling conditions. Inbreeding results in litters which carry many health conditions, all of whom end up in pet shops and purchased by unsuspecting pet owners. Some of these dogs end up being abandoned when owners realise they are not the 'perfect dogs' they imagined them to be.

We were well informed of the huge number of dogs out there waiting for a home, and shelters in need of funds to keep going, so I started Ollie's Barkery to create healthy and wholesome home cooked meals for dogs. Some of the proceeds from the business are donated to fund street dog feedings and other dogs in need.

Our lives now revolve around Ollie. We plan our schedules and holidays with Ollie in mind. We travel a lot less because we cannot bear to be separated from him. We avoid pet boarding places like the plague and only trust Ollie with my mom. He stays with her (and his mate Toffee) when we travel, which also means we cannot vacation as a family.

We have also started an account to squirrel away money for his medical needs. It's a huge sacrifice but totally worth it.

Ollie has made a huge impact in our marriage because of the commitment and responsibilities we have for him together. He has also inspired us to organise doggie-centric events to raise awareness and funds for shelters. We work with lesser known shelters and rescue groups and assist them with their adoption drives.

My husband and I always knew that, when we were ready for a dog, we would always adopt, not shop. And Ollie has proven that we have made the right decision. Our wish now is for our authorities to have stricter laws to protect animal welfare. To make it illegal to breed animals without proper licenses. And pet owners to have more accountability towards their pets.

Ollie is our superstar. A little boy with a huge presence. We have learned so much from him and he has taught us to be much better human beings."

66

Learn to be a responsible dog owner. That means providing well for your dog, ensuring your dog does not become a nuisance to others and picking up after them. Train them, feed them and treat them with love and respect.

Having a pet keeps you both mentally and physically healthy. The unconditional love from your dog and the lessons you never knew you could learn from them will far outweigh the inconveniences and the changes you have to make.

99

JOIE LEONG & YUJIN LIM

#DoYouBelieve InLifeAfterLove

Derrick Tan is someone many people (including myself) consider to be one of the Godfathers of Singapore rescues. I will always be indebted to him for saving Leia from the clutches of the puppy mills. His passion for animals is clearly evident and his devotion to their well-being is admirable. Many dogs have been snatched from the jaws of death or saved from a life of torture and misery under his watch, rehabilitated with the help of his posse of dedicated volunteers and have now found forever homes with wonderful new pawrents.

Derrick is the founder of animal welfare group Voices For Animals and is himself papa to several dogs, each with their own amazing tales.

I first heard of Pester through a Facebook post. Derrick had bailed him out from the pound and was trying to get him adopted. Pester is categorised in Singapore as a Schedule B dog, so it makes it ten times harder to find a family for him. The new owner would have to apply for a bankers guarantee as well as insurance, send him for training under an AVA accredited trainer and licensed with the authorities. He is also not suited for households with young children or smaller animals and requires an experienced and firm owner.

Derrick was adamant that he would not be adopted to be used as a guard dog. There is a sector of the population who think it is perfectly ok to keep their dogs caged or tethered on chains 24/7 all their lives, sometimes subjected to the elements, essentially relegating them to a life of hell on earth. I wonder why these people even bother to keep a dog if it is so bothersome for them.

All dogs, even one that is deemed aggressive and dangerous like Pester, deserved to be loved and embraced as part of the family.

PESTER ZION

When we looked at the conditions, we secretly knew that Derrick was the most suitable person to adopt this dog. He certainly ticks all the boxes. Knowing his past life and all that he had gone through, Pester deserved to spend the rest of his days under the care of a kind and compassionate person.

Pester was found in a home resting next to his owner. The police had raided the premises because the owner had not been seen for some time. They uncovered a heartbreaking sight. They found the body of the elderly gentleman in the house. Nobody could ascertain how long he had been deceased. His faithful dog Pester was sleeping right by his side. There was no food or water, so the dog must not have eaten for days. He was terribly emancipated. Yet he refused to leave his owners' side.

It is said the rescue animals know that they have been saved and will remember that for the rest of their lives. They repay you back with just so much love.

Pester was previously known as Baxter. He was adopted by this elderly man when his previous owner gave up on him. And he showed his gratitude, love and loyalty for his saviour right up to the very end, staying by him and guarding his body.

We have all heard of dogs being Man's Best Friend, sticking by you in good times and bad, and this was living proof of it. Everyone was amazed by this amazing gesture of love.

Pester was taken under the wings of the authorities and brought to AVA. He was assessed and deemed suitable to be rehomed. The animal welfare groups were notified, and Derrick stepped up to bail him out. And the rest, as they say, is history.

Pester shares the house with another dog, Zion, that has a similar and equally amazing story.

Zion (formerly known as Thunder) is an Australian cattle dog that was living the life with his former owner when the latter passed away suddenly. He was adopted by a new family, who quickly gave him up as they could not handle his aggression issues. He was then passed around like a parcel, which must have traumatised him ever more. The last person he was with went to great lengths to help him find a suitable home, and that was when Derrick got wind of the dog.

"I knew he was reactive and slightly aggressive when I saw him, but there was something about the dog that made me interested to adopt him. On the day I picked him up, he tried to snap at me when I attempted to get closer to him. When I brought him to the vet, he bit my hand. I told myself to be patient with this boy. He was simply reacting because he was nervous.

He bit my arm again when I tried to bring him out for a walk. In fact, he would display aggression each time someone tried to get close to him. I took my time with him. I let him heal on his own terms. In three short days, I managed to gain his trust and he was transformed. Deep down inside, he is a beautiful soul and the sweetest baby. His transformation was amazing. He is now so confident and so loving.

I believe there are no bad dogs, just impatient owners. All you need is to invest a little more time and effort and to be patient with them and they will repay your effort many times over.

It sometimes pains me to hear of owners who choose the easy way out and abandon their pets. The saddest thing is how it affects the animals. The fate of the dogs is simply thrust upon them, and despite the betrayals, the animals continue to love and miss their former families. Animals do not bear grudges, unlike humans, regardless of the pain inflicted upon them. At the end of the day, they will still love you."

(L-R)
ZION, PESTER

Pester fell seriously ill recently and required an urgent blood transfusion. Derrick put the word out and was inundated with offers of help. However, Pester has an extremely rare type and many who stepped forward were deemed to be unsuitable donors. They finally managed to track down his brother Baron, and the blood types matched. The transfusion was successful.

Pester and Zion are living examples of undying loyalty, and also that all wounds, no matter how painful, can and will eventually heal in time. With the right owner who will go to the ends of the earth and back for them, they can truly learn to love again.

> **66**
>
> **People who abuse animals do so because animals are perceived to be weaker. If someone is capable of harming a defenceless animal, I believe there is a good chance they might also have the tendancy to hurt another human. Its just a matter of exerting power.**
>
> **I have witnessed people who show no remorse towards causing the suffering or death of theirs, or anothers' pet and are totally emotionless when confronted.**
>
> **If someone hurts an animal intentionally or are cruel to animals, it means that they have absolutely no empathy.**
>
> **99**

DERRICK TAN

#StreetDreams
AreMadeOfThese

Haru and Sora are doggie models. Their beautiful mugs have been emblazoned on a bomber jacket for Singapore fashion label Revasseur. They have catwalked down Orchard Road in a huge fashion extravaganza called Fashion Steps Out, alongside 200 human models. And stole the show. They are also (along with their sister Kaytee) the faces of Wholesome Paws.

Haru and Sora were part of a litter rescued by a Singapore shelter. Her mom was a 'free roamer' who would visit this factory in the Sungei Kadut area every mating season. The rescuers suspect that she mates with the two resident boys there. Each time, the factory would inform the shelter about the puppies, and allow her to care for them for about two months before taking them away to the shelter.

"Haru and Sora's adoption took place a few months after our old dog passed at the grand old age of 18. We were ready for another dog and decided on a rescue. We started to research the many Singapore street dog charities and followed them all on social media. That's when we spotted these super cute black and white puppies on facebook and contacted the shelter.

Both dogs were so similar that we thought they were the same animal. We even picked out only one name that we liked for him!

Malina from the shelter came to our home with two black and white puppies and placed the two round balls of fur in our arms. She told us that she'll be back for them. We think it was a tactic to get us to fall in love with the both of them. Well, it worked and I can't thank her enough for her little trick. It really was love at first sight. Our folks are not really dog lovers, and my mom absolutely hates them, but we were determined to fight to keep the two puppies.

That day in March, they became our babies. Thus began the search for a second name!

No one knew much about their characters at that time but it didn't really matter. We had the mindset that we would work with whatever we had. There was plenty of 'aw-ing', 'ahh-ing' and 'so cuuuuuuuute', with heart shaped emoticons in our eyes, and lots of videotaping. The dogs were oblivious to all the excitement. Sora suffered from car sickness on the way to our place, and slept for many hours. After enduring all the hugs, she found a place under our sofa bed to rest (where she still sleeps till this very day!) and wouldn't stop sleeping! Haru loved the cuddles but could barely keep his eyes open

Our first few weeks together were spent getting to know each other. We popped to the pet shop to get collars and leashes and started basic training right away. We would call them by their name all the time and act like they'd won the Olympics when they responded. Toilet training was also an immediate necessity, and we trained them to do their business on grass. Sora picked it up right away but Haru continues to have accidents till this very day.

We tried to go easy with leash training, and brought the dogs out into the neighbourhood and walked at their pace. They soon associated the leashes with good, fun activities.

One of the things we failed to do and I regret to this day, was more socialisation. When Haru and Sora first arrived, there was a wave of Parvo virus going around and more than one acquaintance we knew had dogs who were defeated by this deadly disease. We decided not to bring them to doggy places to meet with other dogs, until their second vaccination was done. In the meantime, they only socialised with a handful of dogs that belonged to friends. We missed their important socialisation window due to this decision and I really wish we had more friends with dogs.

Sora has an amazing ability to communicate. She tries to speak to us and gets really frustrated if we don't understand her, but she's really good at telling us what she wants and doesn't want. We know when she wants to eat, have snacks, go on walks, need to get out to pee, etc. She has quite a range of vocabulary, a lot more than her siblings, and even knows how to point out which treat she wants to get. More than one animal communicator has told us that she's like a very wise person trapped in a dog's body!

When Haru and Sora were about one, we brought home another dog.

My sister Bibiana was part of a rescue operation to bring two abandoned factory dogs – Mustang and Shelby – from Kallang Basin to Tuas. Midway through the rescue, she spotted a dog running dangerously across the road, hobbling on three legs. She was terrified of the humans and ran away when the rescuers tried to approach her. Bibiana was concerned for the dog and sought the help of the factory workers to trap her. Besides her broken leg, we also found out that she suffered from TVT (Transmissible Venereal Tumour), which is a sexually transmitted disease passed from one dog to another. She was bleeding profusely and needed immediate treatment. She was sent to a fosterer, who could only accommodate her for two months. She eventually ended up at our home. We could not bear the thought of her being returned to the streets in this condition.

Haru and Sora were rather confused with this new arrival. I told myself not to get too emotionally attached, in case she wasn't going to stay for long. At the back of my mind, however, I knew that a dog like her – whom we named Kaytee, after the place she was found - would not be able to find an adopter so easily. We didn't know much about her illness so we separated her from the other two dogs on the first day.

Our first month with Kaytee consisted mainly of ferrying her around from vet to vet, trying to get her cured. Her broken leg had been left untreated for too long and has now healed in an awkward position, rendering it useless. One of the vets said that this limb would eventually ulcerate and get infected because of its position, and advised amputation.

The poor girl was so malnourished that, when she was sent for steralisation, her blood could not clot and the surgery had to be aborted. Her fosterer had to fatten her up first.

All the vets told us to put her down. One of the doctors even read paragraphs from Wikipedia (which is not even a medical book!) to my sister about the condition. That, to me, was the most WTF of all the WTF moments we encountered when trying to get professional treatment for this poor dog.

We decided to pay for her treatment and brought her to our own vet, who promised he would do the best for her. She went through six chemotherapy sessions and she indeed did get better. Today, when we look at her, we are so glad that we followed our gut instinct and are extremely thankful that there is a vet out there that did not take the convenient euthanasia route but instead gave her a second precious shot at life.

Kaytee is now a different dog in our household. She's calm and sweet and approaches us to be hugged. Such a far cry from the terrified dog living in fear on the streets. She is an extremely appreciative dog. I suspect she knew we were trying to help her, and despite the pain, she allowed us to do whatever we wanted with her. That was a huge factor in us deciding to keep her too, because she was so easy to care for and loved us so much for helping her.

Both of our dogs could sense she wasn't well and left her alone, although Sora did ask an animal communicator how long she was going to stay!

We decided one day, when Kaytee was better, to bring all three dogs to the dog park. Kaytee loves to socialise with other dogs, and we were excited for her to make friends. We brought them to Bishan Park. The visit was, however, marred by an irresponsible dog owner and his massive giant of a mastiff breed, who was left in the dog park on his own. He kept picking on Kaytee (perhaps because he knew she had a weak heart and a broken foot) He was humongous,reaching above our waists whist still on all fours. Kaytee freaked out and literally climbed on top of my sister. His owner was no where to be found! We shouted and screamed for him to stop but he kept coming, and we eventually had to use our bodies to try to push him away to save Kaytee. We were really scared!

That experienced traumatised both Kaytee and Bibiana, who still hates dog parks till this very day. And so, our dogs went back to being socially awkward dogs. I started watching YouTube videos on how to stop a dog fight and how to prevent a dog attack but honestly, I didn't think there would be anything we could've done if we encountered another big dog.

Months later, I started bringing Haru and Sora to the Botanic Gardens and to selected dog runs again. They had seriously regressed socially, and that upset me. They absolutely love meeting and playing with other dogs in the dog run but when leashed, they get horrible pack mentality and have the potential to be aggressive! We started training and they have improved but it is something we are still working on slowly.

Kaytee's life has taken a 180 degree turn. She used to have to fend for herself outside and didn't belong to a pack, probably because of her broken leg. She was skin and bones when we first rescued her, but she loves her food now and eats really well. It is very evident that she is extremely appreciative. There are things she absolutely hates – like vets – but she will allow us to examine her all over and apply all sorts of medication.

We were curious about Kaytee's past life and consulted an animal communicator. We were keen to know how she broke her leg and ended up with the scar on her nose and forehead. But we were not prepared for what we heard, and it broke our hearts into a million pieces.

> 66
>
> I've seen enough pictures of puppy mills and breeding dogs in terrible condition to know that I don't want to give these people my money. For the life of me, I cannot fathom how some people can claim to love their dog but don't care about the condition their dog's parents are in, or how they are living. I will never buy from a pet store. Anyway, there are so many dogs out there needing a roof over their heads. I love dogs and I am not a breedist.
>
> 99

GILDA SU

(L-R)
KAYTEE, HARU, SORA

'it happened very fast. The scenes were very scary. I hoped my communication was wrong but I tried again, and Kaytee showed me the same scenes. She described images of her walking into a place that looked like a factory. A lot of people screamed at her and used sticks to chase and beat her. It happened very fast, and it was very painful. Her front leg snapped when a stick hit her hard.'

The animal communicator recounted Kaytee's heartbreaking story. As if it wasn't enough for her to suffer abuse under the cruel hands of the workers and losing the use of one leg, she had to withstand the harsh street conditions in her malnourished state after giving birth to her litter.

Her heart wrenching story typifies the fate of these street dogs. People can be so heartless.

Because of what Kaytee had gone through, Bibiana is extremely protective of her and pampers her always.

I started a dog food company with my sister to raise money for Kaytee's many medical issues, and turned it into a full time business recently. Ironically, with the company, I am even busier than ever and although the dogs eat well and get to go to work and spend time with us, we don't have as much time to bring them out as much as we used to. I hope they are happy and content but as they are progressing into their senior years, I am making it a point to clear at least one day a week for them. I was extremely depressed on their seventh birthday as I thought of how fast they are growing older.

We have always had dogs at home, ever since Shadow and Misty entered our lives when I was twelve. Misty was dognapped when I was eighteen, and we found her a week later, at a vet, severely injured. Her pelvic bone was broken in two places and she was severely bruised – her entire chest and belly was purple from the build-up of toxins inside. The person who dropped her off said that she was hit by a taxi in Geylang, but the vet didn't think so since there was not a single topical scratch. This vet also told me she would heal naturally. At that moment, I learnt that that not all vets can be trusted. A valuable lesson indeed.

We took her to another vet who admitted her right away and tried saving her. But there was little that could be done. My furball Misty was in pain and she would cry, and when we tried to change her diapers, she would snap and, for the first time in her life, we had to put a muzzle on her. It was heartbreaking. We didn't have the money at that time to send her for a surgery and even though we went to a pretty good vet, I don't think our vet industry at that time was capable of such a major operation. Misty died about 10 days after coming home. We were downstairs having lunch when she was about to go. Shadow was with us but she suddenly barked and rushed upstairs. She knew. She went to sniff Misty, and sat in a corner while we said our goodbyes. And then, suddenly she was gone. I was inconsolable and cried my eyes out. We think Misty was probably badly beaten by her dognapper as she had excellent escape-artist skills.

Shadow lived till a ripe 18 years old. She was always in good health up till her last year, when she had a stroke, after which she developed dementia. It was painful watching her pace in circles. I was living in New York at that time and decided to pack up and move back home to spend her last days with her. My sister also stopped going to work to care for her 24/7. We took turns to sleep downstairs with her. Closer to the end, she started having fits and the vet said we had the option to let her go peacefully. It was a horrific decision to have to make, but the fits got more and more frequent. Finally, the day came when we thought we had to do the deed, but Shadow decided to spare us of the horror. She knew we were ready to let go, so she left that day.

I love all my dogs dearly and wish I could do more for them. Perhaps, today, as better-informed adults, I feel closer to these dogs than I did with our previous ones. Everything I regretted as a child with our earlier dogs, I want to do now with this pack."

#IShouldBe SoLucky

I was having dinner with a group of shelter volunteers one December evening in 2018 when Pluto's mummy Shu Hui suddenly asked me an orthopaedic-related question. She had just received a message from a doggie owner who wanted to give up her poodle with a broken leg. It seems the dog had only just broken her leg and the owner could not cope with the vet fees.

A week later, I got a text message from her, asking if I could get a quote from both of Leia's surgeons for the operation. I looked at the screenshot of the X-ray on the Whats App message that had been forwarded by the owner, and was shocked to see the date. 31 January 2018! The puppy had been living with a broken leg for a whole 12 months, untreated!

I realised it was imperative to get the dog away from the household immediately, and insisted we do it the next day. I had a full day shoot with Ginny and Oona and their respective pawrents Eleanor and Rachel, so we arranged to pick the dog up in the evening. The three of us, joined by Eleanor's son Russ, drove all the way up north to Woodlands to the owner's flat but were not allowed in. A maid opened the door and handed us a dripping wet poodle, as if she were returning faulty merchandise. She was cold and terrified (the poodle, not the maid!). "We decided to give her a bath so that she'll be presentable", she said. Bollocks! The poodle was oily, so they probably only splashed cold water on her. They didn't even bother to dry her! We asked for a towel, and were given a face towel, barely enough to cover her ass!

From the depths of the house, we heard the barking of another dog, and immediatey suspected that the owners wanted to get rid of Cherry the Poodle to make space for their new dog. There were many thoughts that ran through our heads, accompanied by many choice words, but the owner was not around and it was not fair to take it out on the maid. Besides, we wanted to get her to the vet immediately.

KYLIE

KYLIE WHEN SHE WAS RESCUED

KYLIE AT GENTLE OAK

KYLIE WHEN SHE WAS SHAVED DOWN

I had a spare towel in my car, so we dried Cherry and wrapped her in that. We drove as fast as we could to Gentle Oak to see Dr Alice. I picked Cherry up and carried her into the clinic, and she clung on for dear life. She squealed when I tried to put her on the table for Dr Alice to examine her, and dug her long nails into my shoulder. Her left hind leg was broken and hung at an awkward angle. Her fur was long and mattered, and her nails were too long, causing her to slip when she finally stood on the metal table top.

We left her at Gentle Oak to stay the night whilst we made arrangements to bring her to the groomers the next day. Eleanor and I picked her up and sent her to June, who worked her magic on the dog. She was shaven down, revealing a body filled with dried blood and scabs. It was saddening to see her in this condition. Cherry celebrated her new look by peeing on the floor.

We decided to change her name, to signify her fresh start in life. Her big floppy ears covered in thick tight curls resembled the publicity shots of Kylie Minogue on the cover of her 1980's album *Locomotion* so we decided that would be her new name! We were all rallying together especially for her, and I made a promise to her before leaving her at the clinic for the night that I would do my best to help her heal.

There was a huge discussion on what to do with her. Should she amputate? Some were worried that the leg had been left untreated for too long and it was too late to operate. Others – including myself – wanted to give her a fighting chance to heal. We consulted Dr Alice, the orthopaedic surgeon Dr Maguire and Leia's vet Dr Nic, all of whom (on separate occasions) were optimistic that the operation would be successful.

After a week at the clinic, we finally found her a short-term fosterer, who looked after Kylie whilst we made arrangements for her surgery. I knew from experience that it would be a costly affair, and reached out to Mojo's dad, Joe, for help. He connected me with the kind folks from Give.Asia, who helped me set up a crowdfund campaign to raise money for her surgery and rehabilitation. Kylie and I met with Dennis from Give.Asia one Saturday morning over brunch and soon after, the campaign was launched!

Russ and Toby's papa, Terry, donated a powder pink martingale collar, harness and leash set so that Kylie could always be stylish wherever she went. Elliott's mama Anna pledged her support for post-surgery hydrotherapy. Puska's momma, Ollie's folks, the huskies and their pawrents and the community of doggie papas and mamas helped spread the word to create awareness for the fundraising effort. When we hit our target in about a week, I knew we were ready to proceed.

Shu Hui reached out to the owner to sign the handover papers, and I registered Kylie with AVA the minute those were signed. She was now legally mine! I could set the wheels of her surgery in motion. With the invaluable assistance of Dr Alice and the fab folks from Gentle Oak Vet, we made an appointment with Leia's surgeon Dr Magurie for the procedure.

By then, Kylie's first fosterer was travelling and could no longer care for her. In stepped Cesar and Chelsea's mama, Lisa, who took over fostering duties. Under Lisa's care, Kylie's skin got better, her fur got softer, she grew stronger and her toilet habits improved.

Kylie went under the knife on the 17 January 2019. We were all at the clinic that morning to show our support – Leia, Lisa, Dennis as well as potential adopters Ju and CP (who happened to be housemates with Junior's mama Cynthia!). Kylie was really confused and hated being alone at the clinic. She started crying when she woke, and the wonderful vet techs took turns to comfort her. I spent the next two afternoons sitting with Kylie on the bench outside the clinic, soaking up the sun and listening to retro hits on Spotify.

When it was time to return to Lisa's, Kylie was overjoyed to be back in the comfortable surroundings of a home and the company of the goldies. She got her stitches removed on 31 January, and after her follow-up X-ray on Valentine's Day, we got the green light to commence her post-surgery therapy. We celebrated by bringing her back to June's for a spa treatment and a brand new haircut.

I am absolutely gobsmacked at how quickly she has bounced back. I am so glad no one gave up on her. Kylie's story brings to mind the many tales of pawrents who did not give up on their dogs, even when all seemed hopeless. Sometimes, we choose to euthanise to make us feel better, to take away our guilt. It reminds me of the story of a dog that Leia spent some time with in his final days. Almost everyone had given up on Qmo. Vets advised to put him down. His owner was criticised for keeping him alive, for prolonging his pain. But his pawrent knew he wasn't ready. He had a strong fighting spirit, something I saw for myself. Qmo was responsive to his environment, he wanted to play with Leia and he loved it best when he could snuggle up in your lap. He was extremely vocal, and would grunt when he wanted his treats. His eyes were full of life even as his body was breaking down. It was obvious he was not ready to let go.

KYLIE AT JUNE'S PET HOUSE

Qmo enjoyed life till the very last day, and finally went peacefully, on his own terms.

I will forever be burdened by the guilt of euthanizing Hock. Could we have done more for him? Was it a knee-jerk reaction? Were we right to decide on his behalf to alleviate him of his pain even if he had wanted to fight and to live? Did we do it to take away our guilt? To make life easier for us? To ease our burden of having to look after a sick dog. It is too late now for regrets.

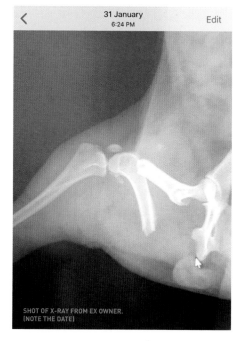

31 January
6:24 PM

<   Edit

SHOT OF X-RAY FROM EX OWNER.
(NOTE THE DATE)

When I look at Kylie and Leia, I know I now have the benefit of hindsight and wisdom to do the right thing. I may not have the strength and emotional capability to do it but I know I have a strong and trusted support system around me who will prop me up when I crumble. I will be with my dogs, fighting alongside them, shoulder to shoulder, hand in paw, when the time comes, right till the very end.

As for the effervescent little poodle, we arranged a home trial for her at Ju's and CP's. We were all worried that Junior would not take to her exuberance. Kylie fully charged is like a chick on speed! After a tentative sniff or two, the dogs left each other alone, with Junior observing Kylie quietly from the corner of his eye whilst she explored the house. We knew that the girl had found her forever home.

On Saturday 23 February 2019, Junior and Kylie officially became brother and sister!

It's not the end of her journey but only the beginning. There is still a long road ahead but at least she has found a loving and caring family, and the invaluable support of a warm, close-knit, benevolent doggie community who will be with her every single step of the way.

EPILOGUE

The most vulnerable members of our society need our help - the animals. They are voiceless and helpless when cruelty is inflicted on them. It is up to us humans to speak up for them, fight for their rights and rescue them.

We all can play our part and animal rescuers play a very important role, rescuing animals one at a time and saving lives.

A favourite quote of mine is:

*"I'm only one but still I'm one.
I cannot do everything but still I can do something.
And because I cannot do everything,
I will not refuse to do the something that I can do."*

Each one of us can do that something to making a huge difference in the lives of animals. Each one of us can become an animal rescuer.

LOUIS NG
Member of Parliament
Founder of *ACRES (Animal Concerns Research and Education Society)*

#ThankYou

How many ways can one say THANK YOU to a wonderful pack of collaborators...

My sincere and heartfelt gratitude to a most supportive and nurturing individual. I cannot thank you enough. Gracias, Terima Kasih, Merci Beaucoup, Danke, Domo Arigato. Kop Khun Ma Krup, Mikka Nanri, Xie Xie Ne, Thank You to the most marvellous cheerleader, **MELVIN NEO.** There would be no book without you.

FAIRUL SHAH, for your artistic vision and fashion direction. Thank you for conceptualising and styling all the lovely pictures and bringing all our ideas to life.

ZAKHRAN KHAN, for designing the awesome cover and a most beautiful book.

RUI LIANG @ Lightspade Studio, for shooting all the amazing portraits and fashion editorials.

SAM LO, for your genius artwork on the cover and throughout the book.

SANTHI and **SARI** @ Binary Style for the delightful doggie graphics.

RAYMOND LEE @ Capsule Productions for the stunning black and white pictures of Leia and I.

TERRY PEH, DENNIS YEO, MATTHEW TA, AD CHAN, JOE SPINELLI, JAY QUEK, BRANDON BARKER, MARION NICOLE TEO, ADDIE LOW, WENDY GOH, SHAINA KANG, DERRICK TAN, JERALD TONG, ELEANOR TAN, LIONEL LIM and **KELVIN GOH** for all your invaluable help.

Many thanks to **DANIEL ONG** & WHEELERS ESTATE; **PRISCILLA CHUA** & CAPELLA SINGAPORE and **JAZZ CHONG** & ODE TO ART for allowing us to shoot at your premises, and for your generous and warm hospitality.

Our gorgeous dog-loving models
KAIGIN YONG, JAMES HOAR, BRYAN YAP, DERRICK LEE, TYLER TEN, DARREN YEO, DANA LEE, JOEY TAN, STACEY CHOO, GABRIEL YAP, ETIENNE KUGLER, TIM TSENG, WILLOW ALLEN, ANASTASIA S., BOGLARKA H. and **LAYLA ONG** from NOW model management, Ave Management, Looque Models and Basic Models.

The fab hair and makeup teams, led by
BENO LIM; DOLLEI SEAH and **ZHOU AIYI** of Make Up Entourage; **CHRIS SIOW; ANN LI; DEN NG** @ PrepLuxe (using L'Oréal) and **EVANDA LOH** (using Kevin Murphy).

Our fashion partners
DEPRESSION; NUBOAIX; RECKLESS ERICKA; WAI TOH; DEHAN; AUGUST SOCIETY; K.BLU SWIM; PINK SALT; ITT SWIM BY ALEKSANDRA K.; MALE HQ; AMOS ANANDA; WAI YANG; Q MENSWEAR; PIMABS; GIN LEE; ONG SHUNMUGAM; theKANG; MARILYN TAN JEWELLERY; CARRIE K.; LING WU; BINARY STYLE; STATE PROPERTY; GUAN LIANGXIAO; LIN HTET OO; ZHANG SHIYI; ANGELINE SOW; ANDREW KOW and **RAFFLES DESIGN INSTITUTE,** and **GOOD DOG PEOPLE** for the doggie accessories.

A very special shout out to **HYDRO PAWS PLUS; SILVERSKY; PAWS AVENUE; JUNE'S PET HOUSE; THE BARKERY, INU CAFE** and **GOODDOGPEOPLE.COM** for your kind and most generous support of rescue dogs.

To all the incredible dog owners and their gorgeous fur babies,
THANK YOU for sacrificing your precious time and for sharing your beautiful stories.

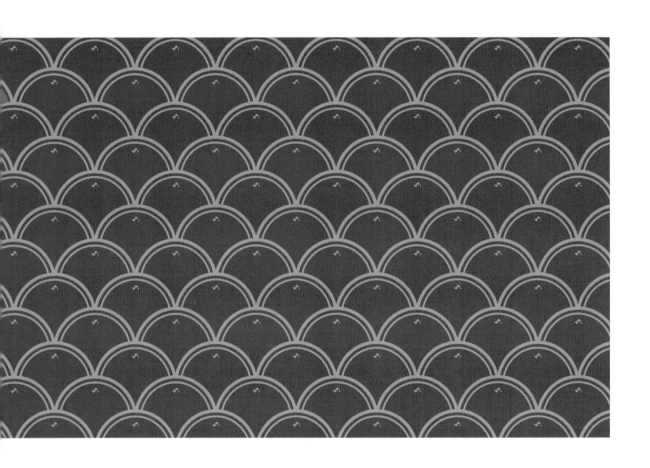

If you have men who will exclude any of God's creatures from the shelter of compassion and pity, you will have men who will deal likewise with their fellow men.

ST FRANCIS OF ASSISI

about the author

Daniel Boey is a creative director and television personality who has designed experiences for fashion events worldwide. His extensive portfolio includes work in the world's fashion capitals, for high-profile clients like Vivienne Westwood, Christian Dior and Louis Vuitton. He is a Governor on the Board of the Asian Couture Federation and his television credits include being a fashion director in three seasons of Asia's Next Top Model. In 2015, he wrote *The Book of Daniel: Adventures of a Fashion Insider*, followed by *Behind Every *itch Is a Back Story: The Struggles of Growing Up with Rash* in 2017

Book design by Zakhran Khan

© 2019 Marshall Cavendish International (Asia) Private Limited

Published by Marshall Cavendish Editions
An imprint of Marshall Cavendish International

A member of the
Times Publishing Group

Other Marshall Cavendish Offices:
Marshall Cavendish Corporation, 99 White Plains Road, Tarrytown NY 10591-9001, USA •
Marshall Cavendish International (Thailand) Co Ltd, 253 Asoke, 12th Flr, Sukhumvit 21 Road, Klongtoey Nua, Wattana, Bangkok 10110, Thailand • Marshall Cavendish (Malaysia) Sdn Bhd, Times Subang, Lot 46, Subang Hi-Tech Industrial Park, Batu Tiga, 40000 Shah Alam, Selangor Darul Ehsan, Malaysia.

Marshall Cavendish is a registered trademark of Times Publishing Limited

National Library Board, Singapore Cataloguing-in-Publication Data

Name(s): Boey, Daniel, 1965-
Title: We adopted! : a collection of dog rescue tales / Daniel Boey.
Description: Singapore : Marshall Cavendish Editions, [2019]
Identifier(s): OCN 1105727314 | ISBN 978-981-4868-16-7 (hardback)
Subject(s): LCSH: Dog adoption--Singapore. | Dog owners--Singapore. | Dogs--Singapore.
Classification: DDC 636.70887--dc23

Printed in Singapore